Wealth
Mentality

Wealth Mentality

Program Yourself
to Get and Keep
the Wealth You Want

S. Ross Ingram

JB
Jourdan & Brown Publishing, Inc.
www.jourdanbrown.com

WEALTH MENTALITY. Copyright © 2002 by S. Ross Ingram. All rights reserved. No part of this publication may be used or reproduced in any manner whatsoever without prior written permission. For more information, contact Jourdan & Brown Publishing at 800-962-6603 or through the web site http://www.jourdan-brown.com.

Jourdan & Brown Publishing books may be purchased at special quantity discounts for education, business or premiums and sales promotional use. For more information, please write: Special Markets Department, Jourdan & Brown Publishing, 104 W. Chestnut St. #101, Hinsdale, IL 60521.

This publication is designed to provide accurate and authoritative information in regard to the matter covered. It is sold with the understanding that the author and publisher are not engaged in rendering legal, accounting, or other professional service. If legal advice or other expert assistance is required, the services of a competent professional person should be sought. — *From a Declaration of Principles jointly adopted by a Committee of the American Bar Association and a Committee of Publishers.*

Library of Congress Cataloging-in-Publication Data

Ingram, S. Ross, 1968-
   Wealth mentality : program yourself to get and keep the wealth you want / S. Ross Ingram.
      p. cm.
   Includes bibliographical references and index.
      ISBN 0-9716478-4-4 (pbk.)
   1. Wealth--Psychological aspects. 2. Wealth--Moral and ethical aspects. 3. Finance, Personal--Psychological aspects. 4. Finance, Personal--Moral and ethical aspects. 5. Financial security. 6. Success--Psychological aspects. I. Title.
   HB251 .I54 2002
   332.024'01--dc21

2002001847

Cover design by Robert Aulicino
Interior design by S. Ross Ingram and Lee Lewis

Published in the United States of America
Printed in Canada

*To the Lord, for His Grace,
to my father, Eddie, for the motivation,
to my mother, Shirley, for the inspiration,
and to my soul mate, Michael, for a love
that motivates and inspires me.*

CONTENTS

INTRODUCTION:
   Putting the Horse Back in Front of the Cart 1

▼ PHASE I ▼
LAYING THE FOUNDATION FOR YOUR WEALTH MENTALITY

STEP 1: **Why Seek a Wealth Mentality? 9**
Understanding the purpose and necessity of a *Wealth Mentality*

STEP 2: **Why Seek Wealth? 15**
Understanding your purpose for wanting to be wealthy

STEP 3: **Why Aren't You Wealthy Already? 27**
Pinpointing specific reasons why you haven't already become wealthy

STEP 4: **Thought Barriers 43**
Identifying and overcoming your wealth blocking ways of thinking

STEP 5: **Belief Barriers 55**
Identifying and overcoming your wealth blocking beliefs

▼ PHASE II ▼
DEVELOPING YOUR WEALTH MENTALITY

STEP 6: **Wealth Mentality Thoughts 67**
Focusing on specific thoughts that direct you toward achieving wealth

STEP 7: **Wealth Mentality Actions 79**
Focusing on specific actions that support your *Wealth Mentality*

STEP 8: **Recognizing Potential Opportunities 89**
Developing your skill to evaluate information that could lead to potential wealth building opportunities

STEP 9: **Staying Focused 99**
Overcoming distractions and remaining focused on *Wealth Mentality Thoughts* and *Actions*

▼ PHASE III ▼
MAINTAINING YOUR WEALTH MENTALITY

STEP 10: **Developing Wealth Mentality Habits 113**
Keeping and building upon *Wealth Mentality Thoughts* and *Actions*

STEP 11: **Dealing with Setbacks 119**
Going from disappointments to accomplishments

▼ PHASE IV ▼
PREPARING TO DEVELOP YOUR WEALTH ACTION PLAN

STEP 12: Problems with Wealth Action Plans 127
Avoiding two of the most overlooked problems with wealth action plans

STEP 13: How Much is Wealth to You? 133
Establishing actual numbers for your wealth vision

STEP 14: Where Are You Now, Financially? 141
Assessing your current financial position so that you can direct your progress

STEP 15: Bringing It All Together 151
Preparing to seek specific wealth building information

STEP 16: Setting Up a Wealth Mentality Club 163
Developing a support system to help you along your journey

EPILOGUE 169

ENDNOTES 171

ADDITIONAL RESOURCES 173

INDEX 177

ACKNOWLEDGEMENTS

"For as he thinketh in his heart, so is he ... ." Proverbs 23:7

Foremost, I thank God for the manifestation of His love and power in my life. When I think of where I used to be and where I am now, I know ALL things are possible with God.

I owe many thanks to those who encouraged and helped this book become a reality.

A very special thank you to the staff at Jourdan & Brown, especially Shannon Peron for her support and assistance in the development of the manuscript and helping to keep this project on track. A sincere thank you to my editor, Steve Cohn, for outstanding work that greatly added to the quality of this book.

I gratefully acknowledge the time spent reading and commenting at various stages of the manuscript by Shirley Ross, Michael Ingram, Nicol Turner-Lee, E. Madeline Morgan, Theresa M. Kulat, Brenda Wesbury, Ken Orr, Frank T. Readus, J. Giallanza, Patricia Waskowski, Eric E. Eugene, Dwight A. Davies, Theresa Kenaga, Jim Oddo, Dianne L. Carlson, Tony Dean, and Andrea Martin-Pieler. I also thank Chadnice B. Wilson and Tamilia Reed for their research assistance.

Finally, I would like to acknowledge and thank the thousands of people who have attended my seminars and contributed to my insight through their willingness to share their desires and struggles. May you always have a *Wealth Mentality* and be as wealthy as you want to be.

— S. Ross Ingram

Wealth Mentality

Program Yourself
to Get and Keep
the Wealth You Want

INTRODUCTION

Putting the Horse Back in Front of the Cart

In 1999, Americans spent 36 billion dollars buying lottery tickets. In lottery terms, 1999 was strikingly similar to other years in two ways: the number of tickets sold was about the same, and very few of those who purchased these tickets actually won anything.

The $36 billion figure only counts lotteries in the United States. It doesn't include the sale of lottery tickets in Canada, the United Kingdom, South Korea and elsewhere.

The television program *Who Wants to Be A Millionaire* was a worldwide sensation as we turned the century. Originally created in the United Kingdom in 1998, it debuted in the United States the next year, averaging a whopping 29 million viewers per night during the 1999-2000 season.

The show has become a worldwide success, with editions in the U.S., United Kingdom, India, Greece, Germany, Portugal, and Russia, as well as dozens of other countries. When a version of the program was announced in Singapore, more than 10,000 people called during the first few days in an effort to win a chance at the jackpot.

People want to be rich.

The desire to be rich — to have more money, possessions, and fun — isn't limited to a specific gender, race, social or economic background, or any other characteristic. It really doesn't matter where you live or how much money you make. People want to have more. They believe the words of an old sage who said, "Money won't buy happiness, but it doesn't hurt."

In any journey, you need something to carry the needed supplies (the cart) and something to take you where you want to go (the horse). When traveling on the path to wealth, money is the *cart*, though most people would think of it as the horse.

This book will show you that you can't reach a destination of true wealth by riding on the back of money. On the path to wealth, money is found only in the cart, while the vehicle (the horse) is something else completely.

Reaching true wealth requires far more than simply making a lot of money. It requires that you establish a way of thinking that promotes and preserves true wealth *before* looking for ways to earn more money, make better investments, and buy better things. A *Wealth Mentality* is that way of thinking.

After you establish a *Wealth Mentality*, *then* you can work on loading up other items in the cart.

Today, more than ever, there is an abundance of books, ideas and available information on how to increase personal wealth. Yet in the midst of having more available information than at any other time in history, we have seen record-breaking years for bankruptcy and foreclosure filings. At a time when there appears to be an abundance of opportunities to create wealth, it also appears that more people are feeling the drain of trying to "get ahead" and experiencing no significant progress. More and more people are feeling the financial squeeze of trying to provide for their families' needs, while at the same time trying to pursue their dreams.

For the past several years, I've taught seminars on the wealth building vehicles of buying real estate in foreclosure and buying delinquent real estate tax liens. I've provided valuable information on ways to use these vehicles to increase income and wealth.

During this same time period, I watched as my personal wealth increased dramatically while that of most of my friends' and family's did not. I asked myself "What am I doing that they're not? Do I just have more information than they do? Do I merely know more than they do?"

Through my seminars and personal experience, I came to realize that just having information is not enough. To some, this realization may seem small, but for me it was a breakthrough.

I initially created my seminars based on the belief that a lack of information was the *primary* reason most people did not achieve wealth. I now firmly believe that I was wrong. What was missing? What did I possess that had enabled me to achieve and maintain wealth?

This book is the result of my quest to find answers to these and other related questions and to use those answers to help others achieve and maintain the wealth they seek. This quest led me to the conclusion that people fail to achieve and maintain the financial success they desire because they fail to develop the proper mindset regarding wealth. I call this mindset a *Wealth Mentality*.

A *Wealth Mentality* is a way of thinking that promotes wealth in your life. It is the *foundation* of lasting wealth because it provides the structure for preserving the wealth you create. Yet having a *Wealth Mentality* is the most overlooked aspect of developing wealth. Even the most well crafted financial plan can fail or be undermined if a person lacks the proper mindset.

This book is written for those who are at a place in their financial lives where they believe that they must sacrifice and choose between providing for their own and their families' basic or higher needs, and fulfilling their heart's desires. It is written for those feeling the drain of trying to "get ahead" and experiencing no significant progress. It is especially written for those who have made, but failed at, specific attempts to "get rich."

This book is not intended to be a substitute for other personal finance and wealth building books. It will not tell you which stocks to buy or exactly where to put your money. It will not tell you which types of investments are better than other types of investments. That is not its purpose, so I will leave it to others to write about those things.

You should read this book before reading another book or enrolling in another course to learn specific ways to build wealth. It is useless, not to mention frustrating, to pursue specific ways to build wealth when your mind is not prepared to work for you in your pursuit. Reading this book will help prepare you to take full advantage of the information contained in those books or provided by professionals on specific wealth vehicles.

For the sake of brevity, I've had to make a few assumptions about you. I've assumed that you are not wealthy already and/or that you desire more wealth in your life. You may have already attempted to build lasting wealth, and those attempts did not yield the desired results. I've also assumed that you are open to the possibility of changing the thoughts and behaviors that affect your ability to accumulate wealth.

Whether your chosen wealth vehicle is investing in stocks or real estate, owning a business, or something else, this book will lay the necessary foundation for you to arrive at a place where you are at peace with yourself financially. This book will help you eliminate the traps that stop you from developing wealth, use the tools that build wealth, implement the habits that maintain wealth, and develop and *Wealth Action Plan* to achieve your goals.

In the following pages, you will learn:

- What a *Wealth Mentality* is and why you need one.

- What wealth really is and why you should seek it.

- Why you may not be wealthy already.

- How your thoughts and behavior affect a *Wealth Mentality*.

- What *thought barriers* get in your way of acquiring wealth.

- What *belief barriers* stop you from sincerely believing in your quest for wealth.

- What affirmative thoughts you need to focus on so that your *Wealth Mentality* becomes and remains strong.

- What actions you can take to establish a *Wealth Mentality*.

- How to overcome the bad habits that prevent you from acquiring and maintaining wealth.

- How to deal with setbacks in your quest for wealth.

- How to figure out how much wealth is enough for you.

- How to avoid some common mistakes when designing your *Wealth Action Plan*.

www.wealthmentality.com

I've also included an exercise at the end of each chapter that will help you apply the information in this book to your life and start and stay on your *Wealth Mentality* journey. I recommend that you start a "*Wealth Mentality* Notebook" — a 3-ring binder with notebook paper for working through the exercises. You may want to add dividers later on to organize the information. Complete one exercise per page so that the information is easy to organize. Blank forms for the exercises are also available on this book's web site.

Please don't cheat yourself by skipping the exercises. They are a critical part of the learning experience that you can gain from this book. Later on, you can use your answers to create and continue to work through your *Wealth Action Plan.*

My goal is to help you develop wealth building thoughts and behaviors. I sincerely hope that reading this book will awaken such a realization within you that wealth building thoughts and behaviors become ingrained in your subconscious and you literally "program" yourself to achieve wealth.

But most importantly, I hope that you use the tools and ideas in this book to become as wealthy as you've ever dreamed.

Let's begin to build your *Wealth Mentality.*

PHASE ONE

Laying the Foundation for a Wealth Mentality

STEP ONE

Why Seek a Wealth Mentality?
Understanding the Purpose and Necessity of a Wealth Mentality

Chance favors only those minds which are prepared.
Louis Pasteur, French scientist

In 1990, rapper MC Hammer was riding high. He had a huge hit called *U Can't Touch This*. For awhile, he was the hottest star in pop music.

The hit sold five million copies worldwide, garnering Hammer $33 million, according to *Forbes* magazine. Money flowed in and out of Hammer's hands like water. He bought a mansion with indoor and outdoor pools, three waterfalls, and $2 million worth of marble. He drove a fleet of 17 cars and bought a number of thoroughbred racehorses.

A child of a poor family in Oakland, California, Hammer spread his wealth around like it was going out of style. As friend Arsenio Hall said, "From the day Hammer had money, his friends had money."

Friends were hired just to stand around on the stage or backstage. He gave out jobs to people for the sole reason that they didn't have one.

Then it all collapsed.

By 1996, he was broke. When he filed for bankruptcy, his debts exceeded $13 million.

Harry and Blanche Mandelbaum of Boca Raton, Florida were looking to invest some money to give them a decent return. They sent $100,000 to the Bennett Funding Group Inc., a Syracuse, New York firm that promised tax-free returns on their investments. Several weeks after the Mandelbaums parted with their money, the Bennett firm folded, taking the investment with them.

The Bennett Funding Group was involved in what federal authorities called one of the biggest Ponzi schemes in U.S. history. The group sold investments that assigned investors leases on municipal and state government office equipment. In return, the investors were supposed to receive tax-free revenue from the leasing contracts.

The Mandelbaums were among at least 15,000 investors who lost a combined $1 billion in the firm's 1996 collapse.

William "Bud" Post of Oil City, Pennsylvania, won a $16.2 million Pennsylvania lottery jackpot in 1988. Five years later, he was broke. During the five years, family and friends borrowed money from him, sometimes begging for the funds. He got involved in business ventures that failed. An ex-girlfriend sued him for the money. And in the ultimate horror, his brother hired a hit man to murder him and his wife for the lottery money.

Hammer, the Mendelbaums, and Post are just three of countless and unfortunate examples of people who developed or acquired money without developing their minds to deal with wealth. As you embark on *your* quest for wealth, there is only one way to avoid the fates you have just read. You need to have a *Wealth Mentality*.

What is a Wealth Mentality?

In its simplest form, a *Wealth Mentality* is a way of thinking that supports thoughts and behavior directed toward achieving wealth. When you have a *Wealth Mentality*, your mind is trained to:

- encourage and focus on wealth building thoughts and behaviors;
- automatically think about and recognize wealth building opportunities;
- compel you to take advantage of wealth building opportunities; and
- structure your lifestyle so as to preserve and grow the wealth you've created.

In other words, you "program" yourself to achieve and maintain wealth.

A *Wealth Mentality* is the opposite of being consumed with thoughts about wealth. Once "programmed," a *Wealth Mentality* allows your thoughts and behavior to work toward building and maintaining wealth automatically (*i.e.*, without conscious thought). Your mind is left free to seek and maintain balance in other areas of your life and enjoy the fruits of your efforts.

So Why Develop a Wealth Mentality?

A *Wealth Mentality* is not a destination. It is an evolving state of mind. We live in times during which change is inevitable, rapid, and constant. Evolving in such a dynamic world requires that you constantly reevaluate and update your perceptions of the world and adapt your thoughts and behavior to those perceptions. When you fail to evolve with the world, you will find yourself left behind and losing any wealth you manage to create.

Money is an inescapable part of our lives. Whether you have a spartan lifestyle or a lavish lifestyle, the reality is simple: unless you're born with it, marry into it, inherit it, or win the lottery, you need an income. You can choose to earn that income directly from your own efforts or have assets that produce income for you. However you choose, you will live with the effects of money everyday.

It is undeniable that America is a consumer driven society, and that the use of money influences our lives in ways we may not realize. We are bombarded on a daily basis with hundreds and possibly thousands of messages telling us where and how to spend our money. We are told what the beautiful and cool, or the smart and sensible people are buying. There is fierce competition for our money and we, as consumers, seem to be led by these messages.

When you have a *Wealth Mentality*, you realize that being led by the hundreds and possibly thousands of messages you receive daily is madness that must be stopped. You realize that money is more than just a medium of exchange. Money is a tool that can be used to shape your existence and fulfill your destiny. Like any tool, you must learn for yourself how to use it properly and maximize its value. If you never learn how to use your money to produce income for you, you will never achieve and maintain wealth no matter how much money you earn. That is where a *Wealth Mentality* comes in.

I have met many people who have told me that they don't need a *Wealth Mentality* because they have made a conscious choice not to be wealthy. You are certainly free to choose not to be wealthy. I can respect that choice. I don't understand that choice, but I can respect it.

I don't understand that choice for several reasons. First, when I listen to the dreams and goals of those people who have made a conscious choice not to be wealthy, almost every dream or goal can be fulfilled or at least enhanced substantially by having wealth. Second, the reason cited most often for not choosing wealth is that these people don't want to sacrifice any of their precious time in pursuit of something that does not matter in "the big picture." I agree that time is precious. I also believe that the big picture includes helping others, giving my family every opportunity to develop their full potential, being able to spend undistracted, quality time with the ones I love, having the resources to pursue the desires of my heart, and the other reasons that we'll discuss in Step Two.

Most importantly, when you have a *Wealth Mentality*, you don't view your wealth development efforts as a sacrifice of time any more than you view tying your shoes, getting dressed, or eating a meal as a sacrifice of time. These things are necessary and simply become a habit for you. Likewise, with a *Wealth Mentality*, you view your wealth development efforts as necessary and they eventually become habits. I will discuss more on developing *Wealth Mentality* habits in Step Ten.

If you choose not to be wealthy, I strongly urge you to examine the reasons upon which you've made your decision. In most cases, you'll find that having wealth will help you achieve the things you want, even if you see yourself as someone who has never cared much about having lots of money.

Now that I've discussed what a *Wealth Mentality* is and how having one can benefit you, please do the following exercise. It will help you see what your personal *Wealth Mentality* can do for you.

EXERCISE NO. 1

How Can a Wealth Mentality Help You Personally?

a. In your own words, what does having a *Wealth Mentality* (*i.e.*, being able to think in a way that automatically causes you to recognize and take advantage of wealth building opportunities) mean to you?

b. List as many *specific* situations or problems in your life in which having a *Wealth Mentality* could be of help to you.

Knowing what a *Wealth Mentality* means to you and how it can help you will help keep you motivated to continue the journey to develop and maintain a *Wealth Mentality*.

KEY POINTS

A *Wealth Mentality* is a way of thinking in which you automatically:

- encourage wealth building thoughts and behaviors;
- think about and recognize wealth building opportunities;
- compel yourself to take advantage of wealth building opportunities; and
- structure your lifestyle so as to preserve and maximize the wealth that you've created.

A *Wealth Mentality* is an evolving state of mind that compels you to change your thoughts and behavior in response to a changing world. It frees you to seek balance and enjoy all areas of your life.

A *Wealth Mentality* allows you to avoid being influenced by mass consumer messages and automatically directs you to preserve and maximize the money you earn to create and maintain wealth.

STEP TWO

Why Seek Wealth?
Understanding Your Purpose for Wanting to be Wealthy

Money isn't everything, but I rate it right up there with oxygen.
Tony Brown, author and talk show host

There seems to be much confusion over the difference between having wealth and being rich. How well you understand this difference will have a great bearing on how well you do in accumulating wealth.

When you have a *Wealth Mentality*, the goal is not just to be rich (i.e., have a lot of money). The goal is to have wealth (*i.e.*, have your money work for you).

What is wealth? Or more to the point, what is wealth to you? According to *Merriam Webster's Collegiate Dictionary, Tenth edition,* "(Wealth is) an abundance of valuable material possessions or resources." Is this how you see wealth?

I define being wealthy as arriving at a place where at least these three things happen:

- You live in a condition of abundance such that you don't have to choose between providing for your family's needs (and your own) and following your dreams.

- You don't need to work (*i.e.* <u>earned</u> income) to maintain your condition of abundance.

- You are at peace with yourself financially.

Real wealth frees you to effect real change in your life and the lives of others. When you need to do something, whatever it is, you are able to just do it. When there is a problem, you can immediately take action and do all the things humanly possible to correct the problem.

Wealth allows you to contribute financially to worthwhile causes, whatever they are. It may just be your favorite charity, or you may want to contribute to the researchers seeking a cure for cancer or some other disease that currently challenges medical technology. Wealth allows you to make this world a better place for those less fortunate than yourself. Doing such things can make you feel balanced and fulfilled.

Having wealth allows you to give your family every opportunity to develop their full potential. It allows you to provide the best medical care and education for your family. Most importantly, at least for me, living in a state of financial abundance means undistracted quality time with loved ones.

This sounds great, doesn't it? If it's so great, why aren't more people wealthy?

The reasons are many and will be detailed throughout the remaining steps of this book. But they all revolve around an unwillingness or inability to live with a *Wealth Mentality*.

In a 2000 survey sponsored by AARP (formerly the American Association of Retired Persons), a third of the respondents said they did not want to be wealthy. An overwhelming majority of those who looked poorly on having wealth worried that it would "turn them into greedy people," make them feel superior, or promote insensitivity.

"Americans have a love-hate relationship with the almighty dollar," said Hugh Delehanty, editor-in-chief of AARP's *Modern Maturity*. "We want it because of what we think it will do for us, but we hate it because we fear what it will do for us."

This thinking is all too common. Perhaps you're saying to yourself, "I can live without helping to cure cancer" or "I give what I can." Maybe you're thinking, "I have enough to meet my own needs and to get a few of the things I want and that's enough for me." Having a *Wealth Mentality* says that this is shortsighted and selfish thinking.

Such thinking is shortsighted because, at its best, it is only true for the moment. It is true for the moment because right now you are able to work. What will happen if you become ill or disabled? What will happen when you choose or are forced to retire? And what will happen to your family if you die unexpectedly?

Such thinking is selfish because you can only help yourself. If you only have enough for yourself, you cannot assist others — including your family, as well as strangers in need.

Reasons to Seek Wealth:

So if wealth is defined as a condition of abundance, i.e., a condition of having more than enough, why should you seek to have it? The reasons are many:

- **To be of assistance to others.**

As I stated earlier, part of having wealth means being able to be of assistance to others. Part of having a *Wealth Mentality* is *wanting* to be of assistance to others. Without this mentality of giving, acquiring wealth can leave you unbalanced and unfulfilled despite achieving your wealth goals. American millionaire Clint Murchison once said, "Money is like manure. If you spread it around, it does a lot of good, but if you pile it up in one place it stinks like hell."

Do you spread around the money you have now? You may say that you give all you can — to your favorite churches, synagogues, schools, and charities — but do you really? Having wealth allows you to be much more proactive in your giving. You don't have to wait until you've had a personal tragedy to prompt you to give.

It is never too early to develop a mentality and habit of giving. Sadly, many people don't give out of fear. They fear they will not have enough left over for themselves. When you believe you don't have enough for yourself or your family, you are generally not willing to give to others unless somehow obligated.

Naturally, the more you have, the more you can give. However, many people with few financial resources contribute generously to great causes without having a personal loss or tragedy connecting them to that cause.

I've had many people tell me that they don't need to give money because they give their time. Your time is a wonderful gift, but if you ask most charitable organization directors what they lack most or what could assist them in making the greatest impact to their cause, their answer more than likely is *funding*. Wealth allows you the opportunity to give more money to great causes and help make the world a better place.

- **To give your family every opportunity to develop their full potential**.

I have a friend whose daughter has Attention Deficit Disorder. For 10 years, she struggled in a series of public schools from elementary, to middle, to her first year in high school. One day, he and his wife were told about a special school that specialized in ADD children.

The more they researched, the more they wanted to send their child there. There was only one problem: the cost.

The school cost $15,500 a year, which my friend felt he couldn't afford. He and his wife made the decision to keep her in the public high school. By mid-year, she was failing three of five courses. They finally decided they couldn't afford *not* to send her to the special school.

She went to the school and blossomed in an environment created to help her reach her full potential.

Wouldn't it be great to be able to make those types of decisions on your family's future without worrying about whether you can afford them?

Another friend of mine was diagnosed with prostate cancer. Because of his wealth, he is able to be aggressive in his treatment and do all things humanly possible to save his own life. From independent research in remote jungles of Africa to small research centers in Switzerland, he is able to travel the world to seek out and take advantage of all the latest developments and treatments. He firmly believes that he would have died long ago but for the information and treatments he accessed as a result of his wealth.

If someone you loved became ill, could you be aggressive and do all things humanly possible to save their lives? Could you at least take time away from earning an income and devote yourself to their recovery or comfort for however long it takes w*ithout being financially devastated?*

You or somebody you know has put off spending the money or time getting the goods, information, education, and possibly even the treatment they need to reach their full potential because they didn't have the money. Please understand that when you put off doing these things because of money, you rarely, if ever, do them.

When you're wealthy, you are able to get and do what you need to reach your full potential without hesitation and without financial devastation.

- **To experience the benefits of having the goods and services that money can buy.**

This one is a no-brainer. No matter what your philosophy of life, most people want to have the goods and services they need to enjoy life fully.

Remember when we would ask, "Have you gotten a VCR yet?" Today many homes have at least two and maybe even four VCRs and we're going out and buying new DVD players. That camping trip at the State Park was very nice, but wouldn't it have been great to be able to fly yourself and your family of four to Hawaii and not worry about how much it cost?

Look around your home. Are there things that you really need (*need*, not want) that you have been putting off purchasing because you didn't have the money? Are there repairs you haven't done because you can't afford to? When you're wealthy, you don't need to ask these questions.

- **To have some insulation from the havoc that illness, disability and economic downturns can wreak on your personal finances and the quality of life for you and your family.**

From 1993 to 2000, the United States experienced the longest peacetime expansion of any nation in history. Money flowed like water through the economic system and people became "richer" than they ever thought possible. They bought big houses and flashy cars, took exotic vacations and purchased expensive timeshares. They invested in companies that had not made a penny. They acted like it would never end.

In early 2001, the economic slowdown was more apparent, and as one economist put it, "The party (was) over."

People suddenly found their stock portfolios losing two-thirds of their value. They found themselves without jobs, deep in debt and wondering how they were ever going to get out. They asked, "Why didn't I plan for this?"

Many didn't plan for it because they were not in a *Wealth Mentality*, but instead were in a mentality of simply making money. Every day, many suffer major medical catastrophes, disabilities and illnesses. The baby-boom generation has found itself caring not only for its children, but for its parents as well. The songs most often heard are "I thought I had enough" and "I thought I had more time."

Wealth allows you to have enough when these things happen.

- **To really enjoy retirement.**

Did you know that only about 2% to 5% of Americans retire financially independent? Why is that number so low?

Assume for the moment that you are 32 years old and earn $60,000 a year. You want to retire in 30 years, when you are 62. Assume further that you want only to maintain your current $60,000 a year income lifestyle in retirement. How much annual income do you think you'll need in 30 years to maintain your current $60,000 a year lifestyle? If inflation is around 3% each year, you'll need $150,000 coming in every year and more if inflation increases.

Now, how much of a nest egg do you think you'll need to have to actually be able to earn $150,000 a year during retirement? With a conservative (conservative at least in my opinion) return of about 10% a year during retirement, you'll need a nest egg of about $1.5 million when you turn 62.

If you're 32, earning $60,000 a year, and haven't begun to save, how much do you think you need to save to get that 1.5 million dollars? You'll have to save all of your income after taxes, and then some. Have you ever sat back and really thought about your future in this way? If you haven't, then it is easier to understand why so few retire financially independent.

I have a relative who is planning to retire soon after over 30 years of service to her employer. She plans to live off Social Security benefits and her pension benefits. I asked her how much she thought her pension plan was going to pay her in retirement. She responded that she didn't know. I asked her how much she thought her Social Security payments would be, assuming Social Security would still be available to her. She again responded that she didn't know. "Well," I said, "if you don't know how much you will be getting, how do you know if it will be enough?" The look on her face told me that she hadn't given that question a lot of thought. She responded, "I'll get by."

You see, it's not that my relative doesn't have a plan for retirement. The uncertainty of Social Security and pension plan payments makes her plan unrealistic. She has no idea if her plan will meet her needs. And the sad truth is that even if she gets payments from both her pension plan and Social Security, chances are they won't. It breaks my heart to know that the best she can hope for in retirement, after a lifetime of working, is to "get by."

Having wealth allows you to create a nest egg that will take care of you after you retire.

- **To not become a burden to your family (or society).**

I've already mentioned that the baby boom generation is finding itself taking care of not only its children, but its parents as well. The last thing in the world that you probably want to do is become a burden to your family or society.

Not many of you would want your children to have to worry about taking care of you as you age. I'm sure you know how difficult it is taking care of yourself and your family without having to worry about whether mom or dad is taken care of. In fact, if you followed in your parents' financial footsteps, chances are that you are not in a financial position to take care of your parents. If you don't change things, your children will not be in a financial position to take care of you if they were to follow in your financial footsteps. When you have wealth, neither your children nor society will have to take care of you.

Now that I've discussed my definition of wealth and some reasons to seek wealth, the next exercise will help you come up with your own definition of wealth.

EXERCISE NO. 2

Developing Your Own Definition of Wealth

a. Write down the first 10 words that come to mind when you think of wealth.
b. Write down 10 things or situations that you think are examples of being wealthy.
c. Develop a definition of wealth that encompasses the essence of the 10 words you selected in "a" and the 10 examples of wealth you selected in "b" above. Leave out any negative words, things or situations that may have come to mind.

It is important to remember that your definition of wealth will likely change as you receive new information and have new experiences. However, by developing your own "working" definition of wealth now, you can be clear about what it is you are pursuing now.

KEY POINTS

Achieving real wealth is arriving at a place where you live in a condition of abundance such that you don't have to choose between providing for your family's needs (and your own) and following your dreams. You also don't need earned income to maintain your condition of abundance, and you are at peace with yourself financially.

There are many reasons to be wealthy. A few of them are:

- To be of assistance to others.

- To give your family every opportunity to develop their full potential.

- To experience the benefits of having the goods and services that money can buy.

- To have some insulation from the havoc that illness, disability and economic downturns can wreak on your personal finances and the quality of life for you and your family.

- To really enjoy retirement.

- To not become a burden to your family or society.

Whatever it is you may want out of life, chances are that being wealthy will help you to achieve it and help you enjoy it more.

STEP THREE

Why Aren't You Wealthy Already?
Pinpointing Specific Reasons Why You Haven't Already Become Wealthy

Wealth building is like using an old water pump. At first you have to keep pumping and nothing comes. As you keep pumping harder and harder, a few trickles will come out. Then shortly after, an even flow will continue by applying steady pressure.
            Larry "No Means Improve Your Offer" Baron,
                                    American entrepreneur

"One day, I will be wealthy!"

Have you ever made this statement? Have you heard others make this statement? By their actions and by their statements, people are always saying "One day, I will be wealthy! If I do what I need to do, if I play my cards right, if I buy enough lottery tickets, I'll get there." It is a natural thing to want wealth. After all, you know it will make your life more comfortable and flexible.

However, listen to the words — *"One day, I will be wealthy!" One day* — some day in the future, there will come a time when I am wealthy. Thinking in the future gives hope that you will get to that promised land of wealth — *One day*.

Well, if *one day* you will be wealthy, let me ask you this: *Why aren't you wealthy already?*

In asking thousands of people from my seminars this same question, I found that the reason more people have not achieved wealth is obvious and simple: they haven't taken calculated and deliberate action toward achieving wealth. However, I also noticed that there are eight main underlying reasons why they (and others) haven't taken calculated and deliberate action toward achieving wealth:

1. Failure to make wealth a goal.

2. Failure to expose and rid themselves of fear.

3. Failure to expose and rid themselves of limiting beliefs and values.

4. Failure to buy the "Gooses" before buying the "golden eggs."

5. Failure to seek out the information to help make better financial decisions.

6. An unwillingness to change their lifestyle.

7. Laziness; and

8. Failure to condition thought processes to act upon wealth building opportunities.

Let's look at each one of these reasons individually:

1. Failure to make wealth a goal

Many of my seminar participants tell me that becoming wealthy is a real goal for them. However, when I ask them to describe their typical day or week, it is obvious from their activities that becoming wealthy is less of a goal than they think.

In these cases, becoming wealthy is a wish or a fantasy with which they entertain themselves. What's the difference between a goal and a wish? A goal is something that you want enough that you are *relentlessly* motivated to work *proactively* toward getting it. A wish is something you want, but to which you put in no sustained effort. With goals, the thought is "I'm going to make this happen." With a wish, the thought is "It would be nice if this were to happen."

Goals come from your vision for yourself. They provide direction for your short- and long-term efforts, give purpose and meaning to your behavior, help you set priorities so that you best use your limited amount of resources (your time, energy and money), and help you measure and evaluate your progress.

Be honest with yourself. Up to now, has becoming wealthy been a *goal* or a *wish* for you? Has achieving wealth been an idea that you simply like entertaining yourself with or have you been proactively and relentlessly working toward achieving it? When becoming wealthy is not a true goal, then attempts to pursue it will ultimately cause you frustration.

I hear a common scenario from seminar participants who are still in the "wish" phase and have not made becoming wealthy a goal. They take a second job or start a side business to have money to invest in a rental real estate property. This is a good thing. However, because wealth is not a true goal, they lose the motivation and quit the second job or slack off from the side business once they have acquired the property. Then, as always, there comes some sort of problem or situation.

For example, the tenant stops paying the rent and they're forced to evict the tenant before they've had enough time to build up an emergency fund for the property. Because their wealth building was not sustained (*i.e.*, they prematurely quit the second job or slacked off on the side business), they have no way to pay for the additional expenses without dipping into money needed for their living expenses. When money becomes an issue for basic expenses of a rental property, the tendency to slack off on needed repairs, failure to thoroughly screen potential renters, or getting behind in mortgage payments aggravates the situation. The frustration caused by this and other types of situations is enough to make those who have not made wealth a goal surrender to circumstances and go back to their old way of thinking and behaving.

Have you made wealth a goal or is having wealth still just a wish?

2. Failure to expose and rid yourself of fear

Fear is the root cause of all things wrong in the world. Fear paralyzes you and keeps you from doing the things you want to do, need to do, and have to do.

The really sad thing is that some people conduct their entire lives according to fear. For example, they don't contribute more of their income to charitable causes because they fear there won't be enough left to take care of their needs and wants. They seek revenge on those who have wronged them because they fear there won't be justice otherwise. Some of you are probably reading this book because you fear you won't have enough money to meet your needs or obtain your wants.

Fear is the silent killer of potential. The fear I encounter most in my work is the fear of failure. Because of the fear of failure, the world will never benefit from great advancements in thought and invention from some of the most creative minds that have ever existed.

Fear robs people of their greatness because most people allow fear to prevent them from ever taking a chance at reaching their potential, and forces most of those remaining to retreat at the first or second setback. Many people I work with are afraid that they will extend themselves beyond their means and end up behind the "8-ball." Sometimes they are afraid of looking foolish.

Some people are afraid that if they actually go for what they want, they might not get it and they'll have lost their dreams. Some have also expressed the fear that if they actually go for what they want, they might actually get it and discover that it is not what they hoped it would be. They believe this would be more devastating than never having gotten it.

One of my seminar participants told me during a break that he buys one lottery ticket twice a year. However, he waits anywhere from six months to a year before checking whether the ticket is a winner. He enjoys reveling in the *possibility* that his ticket could be a winner. For him, the possibility of being a winner is better than knowing for a fact that he is not a winner. For months he'll fantasize about all the things he'll do with the money. He fantasizes about buying a boat and sailing around the world. He fantasizes about living for a year in different countries to learn different languages. He fantasizes about turning his passion for sharing good wines into an international business. He admits to attending various wealth building seminars like mine with the thought of taking control of his own destiny rather than waiting for the elusive millions from a lottery. Yet, he takes no action after the seminars. After all, he rationalizes to me, it is easier to play the lottery than to risk the failure he fears is inevitable in starting his own business.

The possibility of winning millions comforts him in his inaction. When he finally checks his lottery ticket and discovers that it is not a winner, he becomes depressed for several weeks. Not only did he not win, but he had also taken no real steps toward fulfilling his dreams. So, he buys another lottery ticket and repeats the cycle.

I tell this man's story in other seminars and I'm always shocked to find out how many people identify with his rationale and actions (or lack of actions).

Fear causes procrastination. Procrastination causes inaction. Inaction prevents accomplishment. Lack of accomplishment stops you from getting rewards. No rewards lead to no wealth.

Have you exposed and ridded yourself of the fear that hinders your wealth development?

3. Failure to expose and rid yourself of limiting beliefs and values

Do you believe that people who achieve wealth must have gotten it through immoral or illegal means? Do you feel that perhaps you are not worthy of wealth? Do you believe that becoming wealthy is just too difficult to accomplish? Do you feel that a person who is wealthy can't be a person who cares about other people? Do you think that wealth will change you as a person — to make you into someone you may not like?

Perhaps you are a socially active and issues-oriented person. Do you feel that somehow having wealth makes you less authentic?

There was a story years ago about the singer-songwriter Jackson Browne. Browne has been involved with virtually every socially activist activity during the past 20 years, everything from saving the rain forests to getting rid of nuclear power. In a magazine article, Browne showed off his new basement studio, which must have housed at least $1 million in musical and recording equipment.

Browne was stunned when people suggested that he was somehow betraying his social activism by spending his money on something so big and expensive. Browne replied that while he makes a lot of money, he gives an enormous amount of time and money to social causes. Then he added that being a social activist doesn't require a vow to poverty. In other words, he had a right to make a balance between being a good and compassionate person and enjoying the fruits of his labor.

Do you identify more with those who believe that Browne can't have such expensive items and still be true to his social causes, or do you identify with Browne, who believes he can have both? How you answer will depend on whether you are harboring beliefs and values that are contrary to developing and keeping wealth.

When it comes to wealth, limiting beliefs and values turn you into your own worst enemy. They work like fear in that they keep you from doing the things you need to do, and have to do to achieve your goals. In addition, limiting beliefs and values take these destructive effects one step further and cause you to sabotage any efforts you *do* make.

Have you ever been playing a favorite sports activity and had a moment in the game when you played exceptionally well? Did you say something like "I don't know what's gotten into me," and assure those around you that it is not normal for you to play this well? Did you notice that once you reminded yourself and others of your beliefs about your abilities, your performance adjusted itself accordingly?

4. Failure to buy the "Gooses" before buying the "golden eggs"

Remember the goose in the story *Jack and the Beanstalk?* When Jack goes up the beanstalk, he finds out the giant has a goose that lays golden eggs. Jack eventually takes the golden goose, runs down the beanstalk followed by the giant (who falls and dies), and uses the golden eggs to feed his family forever. Everybody, except the giant, lives happily ever after.

Let's try an alternative version: Jack goes up the beanstalk and sees the goose with the golden eggs. Rather than take the goose, which is quite heavy and hard to carry, he takes the eggs. Because the eggs are so light and small, the giant never catches on to Jack's action.

Jack then takes the eggs, sells them to the town gold merchant and uses the money to feed his family for ... a few years. Several years later, down to his last few dollars, Jack decides to climb the beanstalk again. When he gets to the top, he finds out that the giant has sold the goose to a smart investor, moved to Tahiti, and joined the professional wrestling circuit. Jack goes down the beanstalk empty-handed and takes a job making widgets.

Like many people, Jack's limiting beliefs and values sabotaged his wealth development efforts. I'm not suggesting that you steal someone's goose. I am suggesting that your focus should be on getting your own goose, and not just getting the golden eggs.

Have you ever received some unexpected money and told yourself that you should spend it on something from your wish list since the money wasn't expected? Even if your wish list is only in your mind, does it look something like this?

My Wish List

- ❏ Bigger house
- ❏ New car
- ❏ New clothes
- ❏ New appliances
- ❏ New furniture
- ❏ New lawn equipment
- ❏ New piece of art
- ❏ Vacation home

If this looks like your wish list, ask yourself, "What is missing?" The items most people leave off their wish list are the "Gooses" (*i.e.* income producing assets). This is a recipe for sabotaging your wealth development efforts.

Why are "income producing assets" not on the list? Why is rental property or income-bearing stock, for example, not on most lists? In my foreclosure seminar, I'll sometimes ask participants what they would buy first if I gave them a million dollars. Even though they are in a seminar to learn to buy property to sell or rent for profit, no one has ever *initially* said they would buy investment real estate with the money.

Remember the AARP survey I wrote about in Step Two? When asked what they would do if they suddenly won a million dollars, more than 50 percent of respondents said they would either give the money to family and friends, pay off debt, buy a new house, get more education, or travel. Only 20 percent said they would save or invest it.

It seems that many don't value the item that will help them get and keep what they want, as much as they value the actual thing they want. Most people would choose to buy the golden eggs rather than buy the goose that lays the golden eggs. A *Wealth Mentality* understands that this is backwards thinking.

Therefore, make sure specific income-producing assets are on your wish list. Teach your children to value and ask for stock or even a rental property for Christmas rather than the usual toys or other items. Instead of giving your teenager money to buy a car, show him or her how to purchase assets that will pay for the car, the maintenance, and the insurance on the car. Teach them to get the "Gooses" first so that they will always have the "golden eggs."

5. An unwillingness to change their lifestyles

Why would someone not want to change their lifestyle if it meant attaining the wealth they say they want? I believe there are three main reasons: (1) wealth is not really a goal, as discussed earlier; (2) fear of success; and/or (3) they don't want change.

It has been my experience that for many, the fear of success can be just as great or greater than the fear of failure. It seems that people have an idea (whether or not it's factually based) that it will take a lot of work and sacrifice to achieve their financial goals. They also believe if they achieve their goals, it will take a lot of work and sacrifice to maintain their financial position.

Success for these people means a lifestyle change, and the truth is they don't want a lifestyle change. They simply want more money. They want to continue doing the same things they have been doing. They believe that other than the lack of money, they are content and happy.

I'm not so sure they are. I don't believe that anyone wants more money just for the sake of having more money. After all, money itself is just paper and metals to which an arbitrary value has been attached.

It is what money can provide that they desire. These things are usually those you currently lack or need more of, and most often represent emotional needs that run deep. I believe the need for freedom – to explore our thoughts, desires and potential – and the need to feel secure are needs common to all and can be fulfilled through the proper use of money.

Many people don't necessarily fear change; they just don't want change. They are comfortable with familiar patterns and, because of a survival mentality, have figured out how to simply survive within their environment. For these people, living without something they've never had is easier than making the changes and sacrifices necessary to get something they think they want.

I've also found that for many people, the expectation of failure is greater than the expectation of success. To my amazement, I have found many times that some people have even prepared a statement for failure. Those statements start in a variety of ways, from, "You know, most new businesses fail within the first three years" to "There wasn't enough time." Regardless of how the statements start, somewhere within them are two of the most destructive words in the English language: "I can't."

Unless you already have a lifestyle that is leading you to wealth, seeking to acquire wealth and not changing your lifestyle are two situations that simply cannot coexist. Only one of these situations – not changing your lifestyle – will emerge victorious. Not changing your lifestyle is the path of least resistance, and we are naturally drawn to this path. Your current lifestyle is the reason why you are in the financial shape you are in. Until you do things differently, you will never get different results.

6. Failure to seek out the information to help make better financial decisions

Financial planners always complain that people hire them and then give up any responsibility for their financial future. Even if you have a financial planner, a broker, or an analyst keeping track of your financial positions, you have to remember that they are only part of your team and that you must still do your part. It is to your benefit to stay aware of the financial trends and situations that can affect your future so that you can get more value out of the team's efforts. Remember, you will have to live with the results in the end.

So why don't more people seek out the information to help make better financial decisions? I believe there are four main reasons: (1) wealth (or even financial stability) is not a true goal; (2) fear of failure; (3) prior conditioning; and (4) survival mentality. I have already addressed the first two reasons.

Every year, hundreds of books are written on financial issues. Each day, you can walk up to any newsstand and buy the *Wall Street Journal, Investor's Business Daily* and daily newspapers that have large business and financial sections. Weekly and monthly come *Barron's, Business Week, Fortune, Forbes,* and many others. To top off this list, there is a wealth of information on the Internet and in financial seminars.

Most people will not make the effort to seek out and understand this wealth of available information. Some of these people are from generations that have been conditioned to rely on Social Security, employer-sponsored pensions and retirement plans. These people usually believe that seeking out information is unnecessary and is time wasted. However, it is practically impossible to live in these times and not receive the message that total reliance on government and company retirement plans is ill advised. Yet their conditioning is stronger than the message that they must take their financial and retirement security into their own hands.

Next, there is survival mentality. Those with a survival mentality do "just enough" to get by. They know they can get by without having to be proactive with their finances. They may never experience the thrill and peace of financial security, but they know they will survive. These people fall into the "eight glasses of water per day" category. They know that drinking eight glasses of water per day aids optimal health. However, they also know that they can drink far less than eight glasses of water per day and still survive, at least in the short-term.

Then there are those who don't believe that proactively seeking information will make a short- or long-term difference. They take the "whatever will be, will be" approach to life and their personal finances. They believe that if someone's "grass is greener," it is greener simply because they started with a better yard. They ignore the fact that someone had to initially cultivate, condition and fertilize that yard to make it so beautiful. They also ignore that someone is continually spending time maintaining that yard to keep it green.

7. Laziness

Why don't you do the things that you believe will get you closer to where you say you want to be? One reason that can't be ignored is laziness. A lot of people are just downright lazy.

Merriam Webster's Collegiate Dictionary defines *lazy* as "1. Resistant to work or exertion. 2. Sluggish or slow moving. 3. Conducive to idleness or idolence." One of my favorite words that ties closely to laziness is "inertia." Merriam Webster's also defines *inertia* as "1. A property of matter by which it remains at rest or in uniform motion in the same straight line unless acted upon by some external force. 2. Indisposition to motion, exertion, or change."

Apply the combined meaning of these two words, and you can conclude that lazy people, deep down, don't want to exert themselves. And more to the point, they won't exert themselves until acted upon by some outside force. Lazy people may even fantasize about how nice it would be to have more, but they don't want to *do* more.

Why are some people lazy? There are at least two reasons: (1) they choose to be lazy and (2) others make it possible for them to be lazy.

There are some people who choose to be lazy. Why? Being lazy is like using drugs. Despite the long-term damaging effects, there is usually instant gratification, whereas proactively working toward a goal seems to provide delayed gratification. The instant gratification, at least at the moment, is more important than taking care of whatever else needs to be done. The problem is that such moments are frequent and often continuous. The result is they do nothing meaningful to try to realize their full potential. That is why a lazy person will remain *"at rest or in uniform motion ... unless acted upon by some external force."*

A lazy person who has not previously achieved some measure of wealth always has someone enabling him or her to choose and continue to be lazy. These enablers of laziness usually mean well and hope that their financial assistance will provide the *"external force"* that gives the lazy person the opportunity to "get themselves together." How often does this work? Most lazy people don't get themselves together (*i.e., in motion*) until all financial assistance is cut off (*i.e., the true external force*). If you are someone who r*emains at rest until acted upon by some external force*, you must understand that somebody will push your financial position in a direction. The question is: Will *you* choose the direction or allow someone else to continue to choose for you?

8. Failure to condition thought processes to act upon wealth building opportunities

My original answer to the question of why more people aren't wealthy was that most people did not have enough information to make better financial decisions. I found that this was only a small piece of the puzzle.

While conducting research for this book, I found that many people do have a general knowledge about what to do to become wealthy. The most common responses to my interview question, "What do you have to do to become wealthy?" were:

- become educated about something of value to many people;
- save and invest; and
- start a successful business.

They even knew what to do first.

- Attend a class or read books and articles about investing.
- Put money to the side for saving and investing.
- Take a second job to get the money to save and invest; or start a business.

Despite having the information, they did not do the things they needed to do to become wealthy.

I realized that a lack of information or knowing what to do with the information is not the problem. The problem most people have is they haven't conditioned their minds to act on the information. For example, it is generally known that drinking plenty of water (at least eight glasses per day) will go a long way to helping your body maintain good health. You know how to drink a glass of water. Do you drink eight glasses of water per day? Has having this information changed your long-term water-drinking behavior?

From the many years that I've been teaching wealth building seminars, I've come to accept that just providing information has a limited effect on behavior. I now know and accept that lasting behavioral change will not occur until you address and change the way you think. This is where a *Wealth Mentality* comes in.

Now that I've discussed the reasons why more people aren't wealthy already, the next exercise will help *you* think through why *you're* not wealthy already.

 # EXERCISE NO. 3

Why aren't you wealthy already?

Make a list of the specific actions you have taken (or choices you have made not to act) that have limited your ability to have wealth in your life. I know this exercise may take awhile for those of you who have to think back a little bit further than others do. BE HONEST WITH YOURSELF. Give yourself some quiet time and do some deep thinking for this exercise.

By knowing what specific actions (or lack thereof) have kept you from achieving wealth, you can begin to examine the causes of and reasoning behind your behavior.

KEY POINTS

There are many reasons why you may not have achieved the wealth you desire yet. Perhaps you:

- Failed to make wealth a goal.

- Failed to expose and rid yourself of fear.

- Failed to expose and rid yourself of limiting beliefs and values.

- Failed to buy the "Gooses" before buying the "golden eggs."

- Failed to seek out the information to help make better financial decisions.

- Are unwilling to change your lifestyle.

- Are lazy.

- Failed to condition your thought processes to act upon wealth building opportunities.

It is important for you to dig deep and determine the real reason(s) why you are not wealthy already. Regardless of the specific reason you identify with, it all comes down to the personal choices you have made. Once you identify the reason(s), you can begin to make choices that remove the reason(s) as an obstacle(s) to building wealth.

STEP FOUR

Thought Barriers

Identifying and Overcoming Your Wealth Blocking Ways of Thinking

People are always blaming their circumstances for what they are. I don't believe in circumstances. The people who get on in this world are the people who get up and look for the circumstance they want, and if they can't find them, they make them.

George Bernard Shaw,
British author and playwright

In Step Three, I discussed reasons that may have prevented you from being wealthy already. Now I'll discuss more specific ways of thinking that get in the way of gaining a *Wealth Mentality*. I like to call these *barriers*.

Remember, a *Wealth Mentality* is a way of thinking that supports thoughts and behavior directed toward achieving wealth. Two of the most important parts of creating a *Wealth Mentality* are *thoughts* and *beliefs*. I will take the next two steps to discuss some specific *thought barriers* and *belief barriers* that get in your way. These barriers block you from taking the actions you need to take. Once you know about these barriers, you will be able to recognize, confront and overcome them.

Two common beliefs among low achievers are that they have no choice over their thoughts, and that they have no choice on whether to *act* on their thoughts. Their actions, therefore, reinforce their thoughts.

One of the greatest life-changing realizations you can have is to understand and accept that you have the power to control your thoughts and behavior. You alone decide what you think about and how you will behave. You can choose to have your thoughts and behavior work for you or allow them to work against you.

Lasting behavioral change will not take place until you develop a way of thinking that supports the behavioral changes you want to make. The information that follows is not meant to be an exploration better suited for a psychology textbook. I simply want to give you the context in which true change is going to take place for you. By uncovering and understanding what influences your thoughts and behavior, you can make conscious decisions about how to manage your influences and ultimately focus your thoughts and behavior on achieving your goals.

What Influences Thoughts?

Several things influence thoughts: physical condition, beliefs, values, desires, needs, and environment.

Physical Condition refers to how healthy you are. If you are sick, have a headache, or suffer from any other ailment, your thoughts will tend to gravitate toward the pain, focusing on its intensity and on possible ways to alleviate it. However, if you are in peak physical condition, you are free to focus your thoughts on other aspects of your life.

Beliefs refer to the ideas and concepts that you hold as truth. With very few exceptions, your beliefs are a powerful influence on your thoughts and ultimately your behavior.

As an example of the power of beliefs on your thoughts, review the following scenario: if you believe that money is a sign of greed and you believe that greed is a negative attribute, then you will most likely think any rich person you see or hear about is greedy and therefore must be a bad person.

Have you ever met someone to whom you were attracted but did not approach because you thought you would be rejected? Fear of rejection is the by-product of negative beliefs such as "I am not good looking, interesting or wealthy enough for this person to be interested in me." Have you ever noticed how some people with none of these attributes have no problem approaching people to whom they are attracted? You will never achieve more than you believe you are capable of achieving.

Values are ideals to which you attach importance. Values set the standards by which we live our lives. The priority we give to certain values guides our choices for every aspect of life.

For example, have you ever had a boss whose behavior violated your core values? Perhaps your boss routinely presented ideas given by others as his or her own. Maybe your boss spoke harshly all the time and showed no respect for those he or she supervised. Maybe your boss openly flaunted his or her adulterous behavior. Did you stay at the job once these behaviors became obvious to you? Why? The fact that you stayed at that job for any period of time after these behaviors became obvious to you shows that, although you value recognition, respect, and monogamy, you place a higher value on something else.

Values are similar to beliefs but have moral and/or spiritual connotations. For example, if your values tell you that it is wrong to be selfish, then you would feel compelled to share your wealth by contributing to places and organizations where it could be used to do the things you think are valuable. Also, if you do not value selfishness, you will tend not to think highly of and not be around people whom you believe are selfish.

Desires refers to what you want. We invest our time, energy and effort in obtaining the things we desire. Like values, the priority we give to certain desires also guides our choices for every aspect of life. Using one of the examples above, perhaps you continue to work for someone whose behavior violates your core values because the money you earn will be used to purchase something you desire. In this case, your desire for the object is stronger than the values your boss has violated.

If you desire something enough, it can consume your thoughts. This level of desire is like a two-sided coin. On one side, the power of desire can be positive because it can help you focus your efforts on achieving your goals. On the other side, the power of desire can be negative when it consumes your thoughts to the exclusion of all other things, including needs and other desires. In these situations, you will find that you are still not satisfied even after you have acquired the object of your desire.

Needs are those things that you cannot live without. They include physical needs such as food, clothing and shelter; and psychological and social needs such as the need to be loved, recognized, respected, appreciated, or to be a part of something larger than yourself. There have been debates for centuries about what constitutes a need versus a want. In the "big picture," it really doesn't matter. Unmet "needs" can consume your thoughts just as "wants" or desires can. If you program your mind to perceive your goal of wealth as a need like the need for food, you will do whatever is necessary to satisfy your need. People have been known to resort to criminal acts to satisfy their needs. A *Wealth Mentality* keeps you from violating yourself as well as the rights of others.

Environment is made up of the things around you. These things include your family, friends, job, home, the city in which you live and everything in between. If one part of your environment is not in harmony with you and the other components of your environment, then your thoughts will tend to gravitate toward the inharmonious piece of your life. This type of focus can slow down or prevent your pursuit of wealth.

Wealth Mentality Thought Barriers

All of the above items influence the thoughts you have. The thoughts that result can move you forward or away from the actions that you need to take. I call the thoughts that move you away from taking certain actions *thought barriers*.

While there are numerous *thought barriers*, my wealth building seminars and the research for this book revealed ten specific *thought barriers* that most often block the development of a *Wealth Mentality*. Some of these have been mentioned in earlier steps.

The ten *thought barriers* to a *Wealth Mentality* are:

1. Improper Focus

Following an unexpected loss, a great football coach was quoted as saying, "We didn't play to win. We played not to lose."

When it comes to pursuing wealth, most people focus on not being poor rather than on achieving wealth. They focus on simply being able to pay their bills and maybe putting a little away for a rainy day. By focusing on not being poor, their motivation diminishes once they are no longer poor. There is a wide gap between *not being poor* and *being wealthy*. By contrast, if you focus on being *wealthy*, then your motivation to achieve your goals increases as you build wealth.

An improper focus can cause a "survival" mentality. Survival mentality is one of the deadliest mentalities of all because it leaves its victims without hope or even the thought of a better future. Survivalists seek to get through the moment or the day without thinking or caring about the future consequences of their behavior. What may be good for the moment or day is usually not what's good for the long-term. Because they do not think for the long-term, they always come up short. Coming up short feeds the need to just get through the next moment or next day.

2. Procrastination

"I'll get to it." Are these familiar words to you? How about these: "He who puts off things today lives to put off things another day" and "Why do today what you can put off until tomorrow?"

I've met people who take pleasure in procrastinating. However, I've met many more people who are acutely aware of their procrastinating tendencies and they hate these tendencies. They continually try to overcome their procrastinating ways. Whether stemming from fear, not being organized, or feeling overwhelmed, procrastinating keeps you from achieving your goals and from ultimately fulfilling your dreams.

3. Rigid Thinking

How often do you respond to new situations and new problems with the same old ideas? It is sometimes more comfortable to stay with familiar patterns. Even if the familiar pattern is currently working for you, you must be open to alternative ways of looking at the world and adapting yourself accordingly.

Too many people live by the old saying "If it ain't broke, don't fix it." This is a prehistoric mentality that causes more devastation than you may realize. Your way of doing things may not be broken, but there is always someone out there finding a totally different and more efficient way to do what you do. Being rigid will either render you and/or your way of doing things obsolete or reduce your rate of growth to that of survival and then extinction.

4. Overgeneralization

We sometimes think in general terms, and apply general conclusions to specific situations. The real problem with overgeneralizations arises when the general conclusions are believed to be facts, and those who believe these "facts" conduct their lives accordingly. For instance, you could make a statement that since most houses in an area cost around $130,000, you can't get a decent house for under $100,000. The person who believes this overgeneralization will not try to search for a decent house under $100,000.

Overgeneralizations are responsible for perpetuating many of the thought processes discussed in this step. For the most part, "seeing is not believing" for the overgeneralizer. Those committed to overgeneralizations will not change their minds until something that contradicts the overgeneralization happens to someone very close to them or to them personally. For example, someone the overgeneralizer knows and trusts must purchase a *couple* of decent houses in the area for under $100,000 before they will believe it is possible.

5. Circular Reasoning

People often use circular reasoning to avoid taking action. Often, it is given as a reason when the real reason is either unknown or too "unpleasant" to give. An example of circular reasoning is: *Why haven't you increased your business? Because I haven't done any marketing. Why haven't you done any marketing? Because I have no* money to spend on marketing. Why don't you have any money? Because I have no business.

6. "No Compromise" Reasoning

People who reason this way believe there are only two perspectives to every situation — *my view* and the *wrong view*. They do not believe that it is possible to compromise and still achieve their goal(s). For these people, compromise means a loss of their vision, values or beliefs. They usually go for the extreme position during arguments or negotiations with no intention of finding a solution all parties can live with. They adopt the "it's my way or the highway" attitude.

7. Diversions/Rationalizations

Justifying inaction or bad deeds by comparing yourself to others is all too common. You hear statements like "You think what I did is bad? You should see what John did!" or "I only took a few small supplies from work. Jane took a calculator and a typewriter." Some people have been living this way for so long that this behavior has become automatic.

8. Jumping to Conclusions

These people make statements without seeking out information to support or disprove the conclusion. People do this when they say such things as "Mike relied on the advice of his stock broker and now he's broke. If I rely on a stock broker, I'll end up broke too" or "She is an alcoholic because her mother was an alcoholic." Not everyone who relies on the advice of a stockbroker ends up broke, and not all daughters of alcoholic women grow up to be alcoholics themselves. It is always far better to give yourself the time to get all the information you need, than to jump into a decision without it.

When you have to make a decision without having all of the facts, always be aware that your decision could be wrong.

9. Misconceptions

Sometimes you think you know the facts or details about something when you really don't. Often, these facts and details are filtered too strongly through your own and others' opinions, experiences and perceptions. For example: Everything you've heard about dealing with companies in Japan says that the Japanese drive a hard bargain, say yes when they mean maybe, and say maybe when they mean no. You travel to Japan and the first answer you get to your proposal is "maybe." You assume wrongly that they mean "no" and you don't pursue the project as forcefully as you should. They give the business to someone else because they perceived you weren't interested.

10. Ethical Values

Sometimes, your ethics (belief of what is morally "good" or "bad") blind you to the possibility that you could be wrong, or that there are other ways to live a "good" life. For example, many people equate a desire to seek more wealth with being ungrateful for what they have now. They believe that being ungrateful is bad, so they do not seek more. They may even judge others who seek more as ungrateful and therefore morally bad people. Like "No Compromise" Reasoning, ethical values can cause the "it's my way or the highway" attitude.

EXERCISE NO. 4

Discovering Your Thought Barriers

a. Using the 10 *thought barriers* listed above, provide specific examples from *your* personal *thought barrier* experience. This is a time for deep thought and honesty. Try to give at least one personal example for at least eight of the ten *thought barriers* (though I'm sure you can find one for each of the ten if you dig deep enough).

b. Write at least one positive statement that opposes each of your personal examples listed in "a" above. Example: *Thought Barrier: Rationalization -* "I do my job just well enough to get by because they don't pay me enough to work that hard. I would work harder if they paid me more." Positive statement: "I can earn more money if I make myself more valuable to those who employ me."

c. Get out your answers to Exercise No. 3 in which you made a list of all the reasons why you are not wealthy already. Identify any *thought barriers* for each of the reasons listed.

You must keep a watchful eye out for *thought barriers*. By identifying your existing and past *thought barriers* and learning how they manifest themselves in your life, you will be better able to recognize and overcome them when they surface in the future.

KEY POINTS

There are many ways of thinking that block the development of a *Wealth Mentality*. These thoughts are influenced by a number of things. Understanding what influences your thoughts and behavior enables you to consciously manage your influences.

You think the way you do because of such influences as your physical condition, beliefs, values, desires, needs, and environment.

When trying to develop and maintain a *Wealth Mentality*, you will often encounter *thought barriers*. These *thought barriers* block influences that could broaden your views on key areas that directly affect your ability to have wealth in your life. Some of the most common *thought barriers* are:

- Improper Focus
- Procrastination
- Rigid Thinking
- Overgeneralization
- Circular Reasoning
- "No Compromise" Reasoning
- Diversions/Rationalizations
- Jumping to Conclusions
- Misconceptions; and
- Ethical Values.

Take the time to become conscious of your *thought barriers*. Only then can you actively work to remove them.

www.wealthmentality.com

STEP FIVE

Belief Barriers
Identifying and Overcoming Your Wealth Blocking Beliefs

We are all captives of the picture in our head — our belief that the world we have experienced is the world that really exists.

Walter Lippman, American journalist

Beliefs can motivate you or discourage you. The only limitations you have are the limitations you choose to believe in. As a result, beliefs can open the door to success or be a barrier to success. As with thoughts, there are specific *belief barriers* that block the development of a *Wealth Mentality*. Remain on alert for the following *belief barriers*. Harboring any of these or other similar beliefs will surely sabotage any efforts to develop a *Wealth Mentality* and achieve wealth.

Belief Barrier **No. 1: Believing that you can't make a choice to be wealthy.**

No one is destined to live a life without wealth. Those who live without wealth do so because they have not directed their mind and behavior to act in harmony with the laws of wealth development. Unless there were extreme circumstances, you chose the things that have had an impact on your ability to develop wealth, such as:

- where you live
- the extent of your formal and informal education
- your mate
- the work you do
- your lifestyle
- your spending habits
- your friends; and
- your hobbies.

You could have chosen another way to live. You could have chosen more productive ways to spend your time. You still can.

Your choices are limitless, given that technology continues to level the business playing field while bringing global opportunities within your reach. All over the globe, class barriers are being broken down and more people than ever can and do take action to become wealthy. Being wealthy is a *choice*. Your choices brought you to where you are today and your choices can take you where you want to go in the future.

Belief Barrier **No. 2: Believing that you are not responsible for where you are in your life.**

You have no one to blame but yourself if you choose to give in to your circumstances. You and you alone are responsible for your behavior and the consequences that result from your behavior. Regardless of the life you were born into, how much you were not loved as a child, or the opportunities you were denied because of your race, gender or other characteristics, it is up to you to take the hand that life has dealt, and play to win.

A few hours of informed planning could lay the groundwork for lifelong financial success. So why don't more people do so? The answer lies in the failure to appreciate just how important goals and planning are. Goals are the guidepost for fulfilling your purpose and attaining your dreams. They indicate whether you are on- or off-track with your stated beliefs. Planning gives structure and direction to your goals. If you don't know where you're going or how you'll get there, there is little chance of you ever arriving at your desired destination. Accept responsibility for your circumstances and start planning to change them!

Belief Barrier No. 3: Believing that you have no access to resources to become wealthy.

The first and most important resource to become wealthy is your mind. You must develop it to its fullest potential. As you work to develop your mind, you will become aware of the vastness of the resources available to you. From informational resources that I've mentioned before, such as seminars, newspapers, magazines, books, libraries and professional financial planners, to mentors and role models, resources to help you achieve your wealth goals are waiting for you to tap into them.

Belief Barrier No. 4: Believing that you can't become wealthy because you lack a formal education.

Life experience may be the best education anybody can have. If you have a *Wealth Mentality*, do your financial homework, and take an active role in your ability to achieve wealth, you can accomplish more than those who have numerous letters following their names. Remember that Bill Gates, founder and CEO of Microsoft Corporation, became the richest man in the world without ever having attained a college degree.

Belief Barrier **No. 5: Believing that risk taking is only for the rich or the young.**

Gaining wealth involves risk. I would be lying if I said otherwise. Nevertheless, being young or rich has nothing to do with taking the risks you need to gain wealth. Yes, being young allows you to plan longer-term and perhaps invest less with each year to get the same return as someone who starts investing at a much later age. Very often, the more money you have, the more you have to risk. But anybody can decide how much risk is too much and how much risk they need to take to meet their ultimate goals.

Risk taking is for the old, the young, and the middle-aged. It is for the rich, the middle class, and for the poor. The largest factor in taking risks is courage.

Webster's defines courage as "mental or moral strength to venture, persevere, and withstand danger, fear, or difficulty." But I like Ambrose Redmoon's quote — "Courage is not the absence of fear but rather the judgment that something else is more important than fear."

When you have a *Wealth Mentality*, you know that taking calculated risks is more important than fear.

Belief Barrier **No. 6: Believing that living without wealth is, in and of itself, virtuous.**

Someone close to me used to say proudly, "I may not have a lot of money, but at least I can sleep at night." As if people who lived with abundance did not sleep at night.

Do you know someone who has said something like that? Why do some people say things like that? Why do some people look down on those who live in a condition of abundance as lacking morals, family values, and happiness? Marital problems, problem children, and needing to feel loved and appreciated are not issues that only afflict the wealthy.

Many people have accepted living in a state of need and want as a normal part of life. In fact, many have tried to sanctify such a state of living as if it were some kind of religion. At some point in their life, they received and internalized the message that it is wrong to *want* to have wealth. They feel uncomfortable admitting that they want to be wealthy. They may have had no trouble admitting it as children, but as adults, they view the desire to be wealthy as being unclean, foolish and selfish.

Well, it is not natural to live lacking for things. You are meant to live in abundance. Each person has the ability to live in abundance. It is up to you to make the decision to be wealthy.

***Belief Barrier* No. 7: Believing that it's not necessary to make a decision to be wealthy.**

Many people believe that if wealth were meant for them, it would happen. In other words, if being wealthy is their destiny, wealth will find them. This "que sera sera, whatever will be will be" approach to becoming wealthy is the final nail in the coffin of your financial health.

So many people collect their paychecks, let their companies take money out of that paycheck to invest where they please, sit back and let their money "grow," and hope that they have enough for when they need it. This strategy won't necessarily land you in the poorhouse, but it's not going to make you wealthy either. It's a very long road between being in the poorhouse and being wealthy.

In order to become wealthy, you need to be an activist for yourself. You need to make informed decisions about your financial future.

Have you ever experienced the power of making a decision? I'm not talking about simply considering something or believing that something is possible. I'm talking about actually making a decision.

Making a decision separates the wheat from the chaff. In other words, decisions allow you to start to get rid of the useless things in your life — the things that get in the way of meeting your goals. All of your decisions may not turn out to be correct, but have you noticed that just making decisions allows you to start moving toward your goal?

For example, when you decided to stop smoking, you no longer bought cigarettes (hopefully). When you decided to lose weight, you began to monitor your diet and stopped eating those things that contributed to storing excess fat in your body. When you make decisions, resources from unlikely places start to come your way. You start to become alert to opportunities you didn't notice before. This is the power of making a decision.

***Belief Barrier* No. 8: Believing that more money is the answer to your financial troubles.**

If you haven't made a decision to become wealthy, then you won't manage your money in a way that achieves wealth. Often, people manage their financial affairs on a crisis basis and put off the things that don't seem urgent at the time. They consciously spend beyond their means and believe that having more money is the answer to their financial problems. At best, it's a temporary fix.

Simply making more money is not the answer. If you can't manage $1,000, what makes you think you can manage $100,000? If you can't be faithful over a few dollars, why should you be ruler over many? If you're out of control, more money will only mean more disaster because you'll find things to spend the money on no matter how much you make. You must learn to properly manage the resources you already have. Only then will you begin to move toward the wealth you seek.

Belief Barrier **No. 9: Believing you are stuck in your current job or career.**

It is unlikely that someone put an actual gun to your head and forced you to accept and continue working in your current job. *You* made the choice to work where you do. *You* agreed to do certain things and obtain a certain rate of pay for doing those things. If you don't like it, find another way to earn an income. If you choose to stay at your current job while searching for something else, then honor your agreement without any outward signs of complaint. It's not your employer's fault or the customer's fault that you put yourself in your current position, so don't take out your frustrations on them.

It is important that you choose a vocation that you love and that excites you. Those without wealth sometimes make it seem that the wealthy love money so much that they would be willing to do anything to get it, including working unimaginable hours. However, this is usually not the case. It is not the money they work for. In most cases, those who have earned their way to wealth found work that exploits their full potential and gives them the opportunity to express the best that is within them. They're motivated by something larger than just making a living. They love what they do.

If you're not working at something you love, you may have a hard time imagining the dedication and willingness to persist beyond the minimum necessary to get a paycheck. If you want to imagine such persistence, imagine an activity or a hobby of yours that you love.

A friend of mine has a passion for video games. He has literally stayed up all night playing them and felt great about it. I love to play card games and have on many occasions played all night. Try to imagine having the same passion you have for your work that you have for your favorite activity. Imagine that you are actually getting paid to do something you would do for free. I must tell you, the feeling is incredible.

You see, in terms of wealth building, your mission is to find talent in yourself that is of value to a great number of people, and then commit your resources to developing it to its greatest potential. If you're working solely for the money and you don't feel that your work makes a difference, you can change it!

***Belief Barrier* No. 10: Believing that investing is only for the rich.**

I want you to understand and believe that you don't have to be a financial wizard or already wealthy to invest and achieve financial success. Our economic system allows you to invest in wealthy companies via the stock market. Some people, however, believe the stock market is a tool for the rich only. They couldn't be more wrong. The stock market is the easiest way for someone without wealth to piggyback on the success and wealth of others.

Many people will not take advantage of the stock market system because they fear it. They will not take the time, or refuse to take the time to understand financial markets. All that results from this fear and lack of action is ignorance. Ignorance of financial matters will kill your financial dreams.

There are many more wealth building vehicles for you to invest in other than the stock market. I always say, "there are a million ways to make a million dollars." Through your own research, informed thought and professional advice, you will find the wealth building vehicles that are right for you.

EXERCISE NO. 5

Discovering Your Belief Barriers

Remember Exercise No. 4 in which you honestly and thoughtfully looked at your *thought barriers?* Now you're going to do the same thing for your *belief barriers.*

a. Using the ten *belief barriers* listed above, provide specific examples from *your* personal experience of your *belief barriers.* As with *thought barriers,* this too is a time for deep thought and honesty. Try to give at least one personal example for at least eight of the ten *belief barriers.*

b. Write at least one positive statement that opposes each of your personal examples listed in "a" above, *and* at least one action that could support the positive statement. For example: *Belief Barrier No. 3:* "As a single parent, I don't have the time or money to invest in any educational program for myself." Positive statement: "Lots of single parents have managed to get the education they need to improve the quality of life for themselves and their children. By locating and taking advantage of all the resources available to me, I too can get the education I need to improve the quality of life for my children and me."

As with *thought barriers,* you must keep a watchful eye out for *belief barriers.* By identifying your existing and past *belief barriers* and learning how they manifest themselves in your life, you will be better able to recognize and overcome them when they surface in the future.

KEY POINTS

There are many beliefs that block the development of a *Wealth Mentality*. These *belief barriers* block you from taking action in key areas that directly affect your ability to develop and maintain wealth. Some of the most common *belief barriers* are:

- Believing that you can't make a choice to be wealthy;
- Believing that you are not responsible for where you are in your life;
- Believing that you have no access to resources to become wealthy;
- Believing that you can't become wealthy because you lack a formal education;
- Believing that risk taking is only for the rich or the young;
- Believing that living without wealth is, in and of itself, virtuous;
- Believing that it's not necessary to make a decision to be wealthy;
- Believing that more money is the answer to your financial troubles;
- Believing you are stuck in your current job or career; and
- Believing that investing is only for the rich.

You must remain on alert for *belief barriers* at all times. They have a way of creeping in and taking hold when you least expect them. As with *thought barriers*, you *must* take the time and effort to become conscious of them. Only then can you actively work to remove them.

www.wealthmentality.com

PHASE TWO

Developing Your Wealth Mentality

STEP SIX

Wealth Mentality Thoughts

Focusing on Specific Thoughts that Direct You Toward Achieving Wealth

> *Wealth is the product of man's capacity to think.*
> Ayn Rand, American writer

So far I've laid the foundation for your *Wealth Mentality*. Up to this point I hope you have already determined:

- What is wealth and a *Wealth Mentality*
- All the ways having wealth and a *Wealth Mentality* will help you
- Why you're not wealthy already
- Your *thought barriers* and how you can overcome them
- Your *belief barriers* and how you can overcome them

You can now build on that foundation with thoughts that form the substance of a *Wealth Mentality*.

To recap, a *Wealth Mentality* is a way of thinking that directs you toward having wealth in your life. It is a mindset that focuses on wealth development goals, automatically thinks about, recognizes and compels you to take advantage of wealth building opportunities, and structures your lifestyle to preserve and maximize the wealth you've created.

Let's be clear on one thing: all people with a *Wealth Mentality* do not think about the same things at the same time. Each person has his or her own definition of wealth and his or her own goals regarding wealth. Each person has thoughts that work uniquely toward achieving those goals. *Wealth Mentality Thoughts* are thoughts that form the foundation upon which you develop your unique thoughts. There are 15 specific *Wealth Mentality Thoughts*.

1. A *Wealth Mentality* thinks "Gooses"

A *Wealth Mentality* knows that obtaining the "Gooses" is more important than just getting a couple of the golden eggs. In other words, having a *Wealth Mentality* means thinking about getting more assets that produce income rather than just getting more *earned* income.

So often, when people find themselves short of cash, they look for ways to produce extra *earned* income. They take on a second job or do other odd jobs just long enough to fix the cash shortage. This is usually only a temporary fix. Unless there was an *unforeseeable* event that drained your financial resources, being short of cash is a symptom that something is wrong in at least one of the following areas: money management, planning, development of earning potential, or development of assets that produce *"MADE"* money.

I call the money from income producing assets golden eggs or *MADE* money — Money Acquired During Enjoyment. Making money while I'm out enjoying myself is a great feeling. You need *MADE* money to be wealthy.

What do you own that can produce money for you while you are out enjoying yourself or just taking care of other business? Regardless of what your answer is at this moment, developing a *Wealth Mentality* causes you to start and keep on looking for the "Gooses" that produce *MADE* money.

2. A *Wealth Mentality* thinks "Rate of Return"

A *Wealth Mentality* knows that the rate of return is more important than the dollar amount to be made. The return is the amount of money you make on an investment. The rate of return is usually expressed as a percentage of the total amount you invest. For example, if you made $100 on a $500 investment, your rate of return is 20% ($100/$500). The question is, could you have earned a higher rate of return over the same time period with the same degree of risk by investing your money differently? Understanding and applying this one concept will propel you to your desired wealth faster.

I made the mistake of not fully appreciating this concept early in my investing career. For example, with foreclosure investing, my initial goal was to make a certain dollar amount — $5,000 — per property that I bought and sold. I am almost ashamed to admit just how low my per property goal initially was. However, my strategy was volume. I wanted to buy and sell at least five properties per month, which would result in additional income of at least $25,000 per month. I figured that I would have my pickings of foreclosure properties with such a low profit target. I was right.

The problem with my approach was that I would consider taking on any project so long as it netted the desired $5,000 profit. It didn't matter to me if it was a $20,000 condo or $200,000 house, so long as I netted $5,000. I came to realize that earning $5,000 on a $20,000 condo was not the same as earning $5,000 on a $200,000 house. In this example, I earned a 25% rate of return on the condo and a 2.5% return on the $200,000 house. Although I met my financial goal, taking on the $200,000 project was not the best rate of return I could have earned on money.

Aside from the value of the knowledge and experience I gained from completing another project, I would have been significantly better off if I had put my $200,000 in a good mutual fund and went to the beach. Some people I know might say I should've done the same with the $20,000 condo project.

A *Wealth Mentality* doesn't limit the rate of return concept to investments of money. Rate of return applies equally to investments of time. How you spend your time is the largest and most important investment you'll make. Each passing moment represents an investment opportunity to earn a higher rate of return on your (economic, social, emotional, or spiritual) position. Are you getting the highest rate of return on your investments of time? With each activity, ask yourself, "Am I spending my time in a way that is helping me achieve my goals?"

Although the return on certain investments of time is intangible, it is measurable by the degree to which you feel a sense of satisfaction and fulfillment. Therefore, a *Wealth Mentality* seeks to earn the highest rate of return on their money and time.

3. A *Wealth Mentality* thinks "Goals"

A *Wealth Mentality* knows that having goals are important to directing behavior and measuring progress. There are an infinite number of goals and subgoals that you seek to achieve each day.

Whatever your goals or subgoals, you direct your behavior around achieving those goals. Sometimes, the goals may seem as simple and routine as getting to work on time, getting through the day without a confrontation with the boss, taking a nap or doing a personal errand at lunch time, leaving work early or on time, or eating and watching television until you're sleepy. Sometimes the goals seem abstract, such as validating a view you hold of yourself or others, exposing what you believe to be an injustice, obtaining the affections of another, or becoming relaxed. Sometimes the goals are more long-term, such as becoming wealthy.

Some goals, such as those listed above, can also be subgoals. Getting to work on time or taking on additional projects may be part of the goal of obtaining recognition and favor from the boss. Obtaining recognition and favor from the boss may be part of the goal to get a raise or promotion, and so on.

An important thing to know about goals is that they change from moment to moment. For example, you may see someone you're attracted to. Your immediate goal may be to meet that person. To achieve that goal, you decide to go and introduce yourself. Just as you're about to approach the person, fear creeps in and the goal changes to protect yourself from rejection. So, you walk past the person as if that was your initial intention. From there, you will either try to regain your confidence and approach again, think of another way to meet the person that lessens the chance or effect of rejection, or abandon the goal.

You can avoid many problems (*i.e.*, behave in a way that supports your goals) by doing three things:

a. Uncover and prioritize the goals you really are trying to accomplish;

b. Determine, based on your research from various expert sources, what is necessary to achieve the goals; and

c. Do what you determine is necessary (as opposed to what is easiest) to achieve the goals.

4. A *Wealth Mentality* thinks "Focus"

A *Wealth Mentality* knows that the ability to focus on tasks until completion without allowing distractions to overrule is the key to being productive and ultimately to achieving your goals. It is crucial that you do not allow yourself to be distracted by your own stray thoughts or the acts of others. The ability to focus is a skill that you can develop and improve over time. Step Nine offers several techniques for staying focused.

5. A *Wealth Mentality* thinks "Opportunity"

A *Wealth Mentality* knows that even in small or intangible ways, opportunities to advance a position exist in all situations. At a minimum, the knowledge or new relationships you gain from a disappointing experience can be leveraged into an even greater accomplishment. Step Eleven offers several thoughts for dealing with setbacks.

6. A *Wealth Mentality* thinks "Education"

A *Wealth Mentality* understands that the mind needs to be trained to use information wisely and to keep information within its proper context. Opportunities for formal and informal education exist in all situations. Every moment is a new learning opportunity. Every newspaper article and every conversation is an opportunity to gain insight and broaden your views about people and the world around you. The resources are out there. Look for them, find them, and use them.

7. A *Wealth Mentality* thinks "Information"

A *Wealth Mentality* knows that obtaining information is the beginning of making informed decisions and achieving real power. Therefore, a *Wealth Mentality* seeks out and invests in the best information available.

8. A *Wealth Mentality* thinks "Global"

A *Wealth Mentality* knows that the world grows more connected every day, and that global developments affect every person, directly or indirectly. A *Wealth Mentality* pays attention to and positions itself to take advantage of global developments.

I am in constant amazement at the rate at which technology is increasing world integration. I was speechless the first time I received an unsolicited order for one of my products over the Internet from a person in another country. Those who know me know that very few things leave me speechless. When I was told about the order, I had to sit and reflect on the awesome power and potential that lay at my fingertips.

9. A *Wealth Mentality* thinks "Change"

A *Wealth Mentality* knows that attempting to maintain the status quo and keep things as they are is never a true option. Change is constant. Therefore, a *Wealth Mentality* seeks out, embraces and thrives on change.

There are those who avoid or ignore change, in part because they don't see any direct effect on their lives. However, by the time the effects of change are visible or tangible, it may be too late to fully benefit from it or avoid being a part of the debris left in its path.

For example, I have a few business owner friends who refuse to even consider incorporating email as a communication tool. "That's not the way I do business," I'm told. That's fine if their existing and potential customers feel the same way. But, what if they don't? Corporate histories are littered with the corpses of companies who relied on "doing business the old-fashioned way" and not recognizing changes taking place or not honoring the way their customers want to do business.

10. A *Wealth Mentality* thinks "Good Debt"

A *Wealth Mentality* knows that there is a difference between good debt and bad debt. A *Wealth Mentality* may prefer not to be in debt, but takes on good debt when necessary. *Good debt* is money borrowed to acquire or create something that has the potential to produce enough income to at least pay off the debt and maintain itself. An example of *good debt* is money borrowed to expand business operations because the expanded operations have the potential to pay off the debt and provide the company with extra capital. *Bad debt* is money borrowed for something that has no potential to pay for itself, like furniture, clothes and cars. *Bad debt* should be avoided like the plague that it is.

11. A *Wealth Mentality* thinks "Relationships"

A *Wealth Mentality* knows that true wealth cannot be achieved solely on individual effort, and that having the right relationships play a key role in determining how quickly goals are achieved.

Why are some people better at developing key relationships that propel them to achieving their goals faster than others? I have observed and know from personal experience that success at developing key relationships requires finding activities that combine what you sincerely love to do with being at places that give you the best opportunity to meet key people. You have a better chance of developing long-term key relationships when there is a sincere common interest that initially brought you together with key people.

Don't overlook your communication skills. It serves no purpose for you to meet key people and then not make the best impression you can. Work on your communication skills to be sure that what you say and do (as well as your appearance) accurately reflects the best within you.

12. A *Wealth Mentality* thinks "Reputation"

A *Wealth Mentality* knows that fortunes are made and lost based on reputation. Therefore, a *Wealth Mentality* seeks to build and guard their reputation with vigilance.

What's your reputation? What reputation do you want? Are you respected or are you feared? When things need to get done, are you considered a person to whom people go, or one they avoid? In business, I personally seek to have a reputation of exceeding expectations for my clients and being a pleasure to work with. I think a lot of people discount the value of being a pleasure to work with. I've encountered very few people whose results justified dealing with their toxic personalities. Without exception, even when the results justified continuing the relationship, I eventually found someone else who could produce the same or better results without my having to deal with a toxic personality.

Never overestimate your value. I believe in the biblical instruction that says "seek and ye shall find." If your customers, colleagues, friends, or loved ones seek, they will eventually find someone to fill the need you currently satisfy.

13. A *Wealth Mentality* thinks "Competition"

A *Wealth Mentality* knows that there is always someone who wants what they have. This is not living in a state of paranoia. Instead, it is a realization that competition for everything is fierce. Therefore, a *Wealth Mentality* takes care of what they have and keeps a watchful eye to identify, monitor, and stay far ahead of the competition.

14. A *Wealth Mentality* thinks "Negotiation"

A *Wealth Mentality* knows that negotiation is a part of everyday life and that the ability to negotiate effectively and efficiently parallels with the ability to achieve goals. Therefore, a *Wealth Mentality* proactively seeks to improve negotiation skills so that they may advance their own interest while maintaining positive, long-term relationships that serves them in the future. You never know if and when you will have to cross the other side's path again.

www.wealthmentality.com

15. A *Wealth Mentality* thinks "Checks and Balances"

A *Wealth Mentality* knows there is a fine line between becoming confident in a vision based on early successes and arrogantly believing that a vision is flawless. Therefore, a *Wealth Mentality* puts a system of "checks and balances" in place to be on alert for signs of arrogance and to force a periodic reexamination of the vision.

 # EXERCISE NO. 6

Focusing on Wealth Mentality Thoughts

For fifteen consecutive days, focus on a different *Wealth Mentality Thought* each day. Throughout the day, think of ways to apply that thought to all aspects of your life.

For example, for one full day, focus on "Rate of Return" or "Change." Paraphrase the thought for yourself on an index card or small piece of paper that you keep with you and read several times throughout the day. You can write, "A *Wealth Mentality* focuses on the rate of return and not just income" or "A *Wealth Mentality* embraces change."

For "Rate of Return," look at all your investments of time and money to be sure you are getting the best rate of return you can. For "Change," pay more attention to your thoughts and actions to determine whether you are avoiding or embracing change.

By continuing to repeat this process, you will be able to focus on each *Wealth Mentality Thought* for a full day at least twice a month.

KEY POINTS

A *Wealth Mentality* is a way of thinking that directs you toward having wealth in your life. Since all people have their own personal definition of wealth, it follows that each person would have unique thoughts that help them develop their wealth goals.

Wealth Mentality Thoughts form the foundation upon which you develop the thoughts that help you achieve your wealth goals. A *Wealth Mentality* thinks:

- "Gooses"
- "Rate of Return"
- "Goals"
- "Concentration"
- "Opportunity"
- "Education"
- "Information"
- "Global"
- "Change"
- "Good Debt"
- "Relationships"
- "Reputation"
- "Competition"
- "Negotiation"
- "Checks and Balances"

STEP SEVEN
Wealth Mentality Actions
Focusing on Specific Actions that Support Your Wealth Mentality

He becometh poor that dealeth with a slack hand: but the hand of the diligent maketh rich.

Proverbs 10:4

Up to this point, I have been talking a great deal about the thoughts that block, as well as thoughts that form the substance of a *Wealth Mentality*. In this Step, I will recommend certain actions that you can do to support your *Wealth Mentality* and to make it start to work for you. I call these actions *Wealth Mentality Actions*.

Wealth Mentality Actions are those that reinforce *Wealth Mentality Thoughts* and provide the information and motivation to achieve your wealth development goals. Without daily reinforcement, *Wealth Mentality Thoughts* will not have the support they need to become and remain a part of your conscious thought processes, and ultimately affect your behavior.

Start with these:

1. Read a financial newspaper or personal finance magazine every day.

I've said this before and I'll say it again: there is an enormous amount of information out there that you can use to learn about increasing your wealth. You can choose from these and many others: *The Wall Street Journal, Investor's Business Daily, BusinessWeek, Fortune, Forbes, Barron's, Money, The New York Times business section, Kiplinger's Personal Finance,* and so many more newsletters, business journals, internet sites, e-zines and internet subscriptions.

Reading well known financial periodicals is necessary because it is important to know what your competition and your customers already know. However, reading what everyone else is reading only helps you keep up with everyone else. To exceed expectations and achieve extraordinary results, you must find lesser known and more exclusive sources of information. Among the best sources of information I have found to gain insight and broaden my perspective about the American economy are foreign-produced periodicals.

Some foreign produced periodicals include: *The Financial Post, The Financial Times, The Economist, Far Eastern Economic Review, Financial World,* and of course, the international versions of *The Wall Street Journal.* These and other foreign publications can be purchased at some local newsstands or independent bookstores and at major bookstore chains. Additional sources for domestic and foreign business periodicals are available on this book's web site.

2. Read a business or finance book every month.

Make book reading a habit. It is one of the best ways to get complete and thorough information about finances and investment strategies. Newspaper and magazine articles are wonderful, but they have limited space for the information they provide. Seminars and workshops provide lots of information, but use a combination of communication techniques, including reading, writing, and oral skills. Only in books do you get the details and thoroughness of a seminar combined with the portability of the magazine or newspaper article.

You can't read every book out there, but you can read at least one book a month. If you can read two-a-month, even better. If your reading time is limited, many of these books (especially the best sellers) are on audiotape. Listen to the books in your car or on the plane.

Naturally, reading entire books is better. But if you have limited time to read the hundreds of financial and business books published each month, you can get monthly newsletters that summarize them. Visit this book's web site if you want reading recommendations and summaries.

3. Attend seminars, both classroom and Internet.

It used to be that the rich went to their advisors and discussed money. The rest of the population had little access to the experts who knew how to turn time into money and money into wealth. Now, there is almost always a seminar somewhere providing the information you need to get what you want.

Why are good seminars so valuable? They keep you from having to reinvent the wheel, so to speak. When you need specialized information or a proven "system," the best seminars not only save you time by providing you with the information you need in one concise package, but they take years off your learning curve by giving you insight from personal experiences. The insight you gain can help you avoid common mistakes and give you tools that help you achieve your goals more quickly.

You may attend different seminars where different speakers give you different and sometimes conflicting opinions on the same matter. That's okay. The more opinions and information you have, the better your decisions will be.

I generally find that every seminar I attend has at least one idea that I can implement to improve some aspect of my business or personal life. Sometimes, all it takes is one idea to revolutionize the way you view the world or conduct your business. One idea can catapult you years ahead of where you thought you would be. So, find out what you need to know, and work to learn it. Find out who is giving the seminar, check out his or her background (or the background of the sponsoring organization), and if it seems that the speaker has something to offer, GO!

4. Practice analyzing business situations.

I believe that analyzing business situations, even just for practice, is so important that I made it a regular feature in a newsletter, *The Strategic Thinker* (www.thestrategicthinker.com), published by one of my companies. Although the newsletter is primarily read by CEOs and senior corporation management, it can help any individual looking to develop critical thinking skills. The "Strategic Problem Solving" feature proposes some sort of business problem in each issue. Readers can send in how they would handle the problem. The goal is to regularly exercise your thinking skills. The newsletter does not provide a right or wrong solution to the problem. Instead, it raises questions that help you consider the long-range implications of certain responses to the problem.

You don't have to subscribe to the newsletter to practice analyzing business situations. You can do this type of exercise by reading any financial newspaper. There is always a story of a company that is struggling or experiencing a decrease in their stock for one reason or another. You can evaluate how you might respond to that company's problem. I understand that you won't have full information about the company's situation, but then again, you usually don't have full information about real problems either. The goal is to keep your thinking skills sharp and ready to take action when you encounter actual problems.

5. Learn about different kinds of "Gooses."

I always say that there are a million ways to make a million dollars. Every thing around you is someone's goose. From toothpicks to the canisters sitting on your kitchen counter to the "grass" in Easter baskets, someone receives income from the sale of these items.

Start learning about different kinds of income producing assets, from real estate to pork belly futures. Overlook nothing. You never know what may interest you or spark some insight that will help you develop assets from scratch, or acquire existing assets.

Remember that true assets produce *MADE* Money that you can live off of or use to acquire more assets.

6. Become a student of tax strategy.

It's not just how much you make, but how much you keep. Never pay more than required. If you're paying the federal and state governments more than required, ask yourself: is it because of *fear* or *ignorance?* Either reason is unacceptable to someone who has a *Wealth Mentality.*

Take the time to read everything you can on strategies you can use to legitimately help you keep more of your money. A great tax advisor and/or tax lawyer is an invaluable resource for helping you structure your lifestyle and transactions to take full advantage of tax rules and regulations. From forming corporations and partnerships to establishing tax-free exchanges, great tax professionals should always cost you less than you will save by using their advice. Ask people you respect for the names of professionals they respect.

7. Keep a picture of your goals "in front of you."

Keep your eye on what you want. I mean this literally. Keep a picture of what ever it is you seek near you so that you can draw inspiration from it.

A seminar participant told me one great way to do this. She made a collage of all that she visioned for herself. The collage is custom framed and comprised of pictures from magazines, pictures she had taken, and drawings she did. She keeps it on the wall in her office. She doesn't mind explaining her vision to any co-worker who asks. Some of her co-workers actually think it is a piece of art she purchased. I guess in some ways it is a piece of art.

I also recommend that you get out and regularly view the real thing up close when possible. Seeing what you want up close as opposed to just looking at pictures in magazines provides a different level of inspiration. If someone else was able to achieve it, then it is possible for you, too.

8. Practice patience.

Patience is not only a virtue, but a cornerstone in the development of lasting wealth. Instant success or wealth is only truly useful when you are prepared to deal with it. Otherwise, it can be squandered and leave overwhelming feelings of regret. Just remember the stories of Hammer, the Mendelbaums, and Post in Step One.

You must find your own activity that proactively provides you with the opportunity to practice patience. Gardening provides this for me. With gardening, I learn that things do not grow the way they're expected to unless I provide the proper conditions. It can be exhausting work just to provide the proper conditions, and even then, there are no guarantees that my plants will grow as expected.

Trying too hard to accelerate the growth process can sometimes leave the plants in "shock" and do more harm than good. I start some plants from seed and it may take years for them to mature into what I want them to be. Other plants I buy already mature. However, it may still take quite some time for the plants to adjust to their new surroundings and to get to the point where they require little or no maintenance. I buy other plants to provide me with the color I need to complete my vision or to provide instant filler until the other plants grow and mature. In the end, the sense of pride, accomplishment and enjoyment I get makes it worth all the effort.

The same is true with wealth development. You must give your wealth the opportunity to grow by creating the proper conditions and maintaining your plan. It can be exhausting work at times, and there are no guarantees that things will turn out as you expect them to. However, I can tell you that the surprises, and the sense of pride, accomplishment and enjoyment you will experience along the way makes the ride worth it.

I must give a few words of caution regarding *Wealth Mentality Actions*. Do not make it a point of *Wealth Mentality Actions* to simply get as much financial information as possible. Trying to get as much financial information as possible leads to information overload. Information overload causes the opposite of the intended effect. Instead of reinforcing *Wealth Mentality Thoughts* and helping you achieve your wealth goals, information overload causes paralysis of thought processes and productive behavior.

Make it a point of *Wealth Mentality Actions* to learn *what to do* with the *best* information you can get to advance your position. Trying to follow all of the "hot tips" and other advice from the thousands of "experts" promoted daily by the media can cause you to lose focus. Implementing *Wealth Mentality Actions* ultimately will direct you to a few key sources of information that you can use as part of *your* continuing financial education. Having a few quality sources of information to draw on will help you avoid information overload and keep you moving toward achieving your wealth goals.

Step Eight will help you to evaluate the information you receive so that you can decide what represents potential wealth building opportunities for you.

EXERCISE NO. 7

Start Taking Action Now

Get out your calendar right now (or make one right now) and actually schedule a time to do at least one (preferably more than one) of the *Wealth Mentality Actions*. Don't forget to schedule time for preliminary tasks as well. For example, if you're going to start reading a financial periodical every day or begin reading a book a month, you need to schedule time to select and acquire the periodical or book.

By starting right now, you are making a deadly strike against procrastination and a great step toward achieving your wealth goals.

KEY POINTS

Wealth Mentality Thoughts must be reinforced daily with *Wealth Mentality Actions*. This reinforcement will help *Wealth Mentality Thoughts* become and remain a part of your conscious thought processes so that you will continue to do the things that are necessary to achieve your wealth goals.

The eight *Wealth Mentality Actions* to start with are:

1. Read a financial newspaper or personal finance magazine every day.
2. Read a business or finance book every month.
3. Attend seminars, both classroom and Internet.
4. Practice analyzing business situations.
5. Learn about different kinds of "Gooses."
6. Become a student of tax strategy.
7. Keep a picture of your goals "in front of you"
8. Practice patience.

Wealth Mentality Actions beyond the eight above will depend upon the specific wealth building vehicles(s) you ultimately select.

STEP EIGHT

Recognizing Potential Opportunities

Developing Your Skill to Evaluate Information that Could Lead to Potential Wealth Building Opportunities

> *Opportunity is missed by most people because it is dressed in overalls and looks like work.*
> Thomas Edison, American inventor

How many opportunities have you allowed to pass you by because you didn't want to do the work? Whether the work was mental or physical, maybe you didn't compel yourself to do the work because you didn't recognize the true potential of the opportunity before you. Part of having a *Wealth Mentality* is being able to evaluate information and recognize wealth building opportunities. As you gain confidence in your evaluation skills and your ability to recognize potential opportunities, your *Wealth Mentality* will compel you to take advantage of those opportunities.

Let me give you "food for thought" to help you evaluate and recognize potential opportunities. Since there is no one standard by which to evaluate investments, I intend that the questions to follow will be your starting point.

Your goals and tolerance for risk require that you personalize every evaluation. You can make comparisons to reveal how a potential investment measures up to its competition, or how it measures up within its industry. However, though it is an essential part of a thorough analysis, "doing the numbers" and making comparisons will only tell you what everyone else can just as easily find out. Ultimately, it is your insight that allows you to see potential where others don't. Therefore, work to develop and become confident in applying your insight to estimate an investment's potential. Sometimes you'll be right and sometimes you'll be wrong. With diligent practice, you'll be right far more often.

There are six categories of questions to consider before disregarding or proceeding with an investment. They are pre-evaluation, evaluating the opportunity and its industry, making comparisons, evaluating growth potential, developing your insight, and determining if it's a goose with golden eggs. Each of these categories should be a subject for you to explore in greater detail as part of the education program I'll discuss in Step Fifteen. The whole point to these questions is to get you thinking – thinking about the existence of an opportunity as well as its growth and downward potential.

Let's look at the questions you need to ask in each of the six categories.

Pre-evaluation Questions

- What do you already know about the type of investment and the specific investment?

- How much time would it take to thoroughly investigate the investment?

- Is there enough time to research the investment and still earn a rate of return that is equal to or greater than that received from your current investments?

Evaluating the Opportunity and Its Industry

- What is the price comprised of?
- How was the price arrived at?
- What is the price a reflection of?
- Is there an industry standard for determining the price and how does this price compare to the industry standard?
- Who needs what the opportunity is selling?
- How stable (financially, politically) and loyal (their mentality) is this market?
- Can they get what they need from another source?
- If so, how much more or less would it cost them to get it from another source?
- How much sooner or later would it take them to get it from another source?
- Does this idea take advantage of shifts (social, cultural, economic, demographic)?
- What is the initial investment?
- What does the initial investment control? Would it be controlling something of greater value than the initial investment?
- How long will it take to produce income for you?
- What is the expected short- and long-term appreciation of the investment?
- What is the level of risk? How is that risk level determined?

- What will have to occur for the investment to produce as expected? How likely is it that those events will occur? What could prevent the events from occurring? How likely is it that what could prevent the events from occurring will occur?

- What will have to occur for the investment to lose all of its value? How likely is it that those events will occur?

- How quickly could you sell it if you had to?

Making Comparisons

If the potential opportunity is an existing business, you can use ratios and other evaluations to measure the company's performance and potential for growth. If a company's performance is followed by a financial organization, it can be more efficient to use calculations and evaluations they provide as a starting point. For more speculative investments, you will have to do the calculations and evaluations for yourself (which is usually best) since these types of investments aren't as popular, and as such aren't followed.

Just as you will do for your personal finances in Step Thirteen, you must look at such fundamentals as revenue, earnings, expenses and cash flow for potential opportunities. To calculate the numbers, you will need certain information about the company. This you can get from a variety of sources, such as financial periodicals, web sites, brokerages and other financial institutions, annual reports and other information from the company, and from the Securities Exchange Commission. With this information, answer the following:

- What is the company's net earnings (profits after all expenses) growth rate? How does it compare to its competitors and the industry as a whole?

- What are the company's earnings per share (net earnings for the past four quarters divided by the number of common shares outstanding)? How does it compare to its competitors and the industry as a whole?

- What is the company's price to earnings ratio (current market price of its stock divided by earnings per share)? How does it compare to its competitors and the industry as a whole?

- What is the background and experience of those who will be managing the day-to-day operations?

- What is the background and experience of those who will be advising the operating management?

- Who are the company's biggest competitors?

- Is the industry made up of three or four major companies and several boutique operations, or are there more than three or four majors?

- Where does the company stand in the larger industry picture? Is it at the top? Second? Third? Is it an up-and-coming company?

- What differentiates it from its competitors? What do its competitors offer that it doesn't? What does it offer that its competitors don't?

- Does the company have a niche in the marketplace? What is it known for?

- What share of the market does it command?

- How established is the company? How established are their competitors?

- Does this company have a valuable brand name?

- Is the industry growing, diminishing, or standing pat? Why?

- Does the technology have room for growth? How soon is a competitor likely to come up with new technology that will reduce the value of this technology and/or change the structure of the industry?

- How good is the company's reputation for product and/or service? How good is its main competitor's reputation?

It is important to remember that no one ratio or other factor, such as management, presents the whole picture of a company's value. Therefore, learn to use as many different ratios and other factors as possible when making comparisons. Additional information on how to use the ratios discussed, as well as other ratios and calculations, are available on this book's web site.

Evaluating Growth Potential

- What "life event" does the product or service address?

- Does the product or service address the life event as a whole or just one part of the event?

- Are there beneficial alliances that could be formed to serve the customer better?

- Does it operate in an open market?

- Is there a mix of human contact and electronic information?

- How does it use the latest technology to add value to that information for customers?

- Can you effectively and efficiently add value to it without substantially increasing cost?

Developing Your Insight

Insight is the understanding, wisdom and intuition you bring to a situation. It is the result of your experience, your ability and willingness to consider alternative ways of viewing the world, and exploring the deepest levels of your thoughts and creativity. Filling in the blank to these questions with as many things as you can is a great way to start exploring your thoughts and creativity regarding a potential opportunity.

- "I could reap huge benefits from this investment *if* _____."
- "This investment would be a great project *if* _____."
- How can you bring about the *"if"* in the previous two questions or substitute something just as good?
- What assumptions are you making about the investment?
- What if you're wrong about the assumptions you've made?
- What would be a better solution for this market?
- What would be necessary to bring about the better solution for this market?
- Who (an existing business) or what type of business has the capability of bringing the components together and manufacturing this better solution?
- How soon is the competition likely to realize that they can bring the components together and manufacture this better solution?
- How long would it take them to bring the components together and manufacture this better solution once they realize that they can?

- Can I bring the components together and manufacture this better solution?

- Is it worth it for me to bring the components together and manufacture this better solution?

Is This a Goose and Are Its Eggs Golden?

Remember when I spoke about the "Gooses" and the golden eggs? Ultimately, your evaluation is seeking to answer the question, "Is this a goose with golden eggs?"

It is a goose if the investment can repeatedly produce results. It is not a goose if it is a one-time or one-shot deal.

The eggs are golden if the result produced by the investment is income that can be reinvested to produce more income or used to satisfy your lifestyle expenses. The eggs are not golden if the income must be reinvested just to maintain the existence of the investment.

If you want to proceed with the opportunity after answering the questions above, then finally ask yourself, "Is there something else that I can invest in right now that would give me the same or a better rate of return, given my goals and tolerance for risk?"

Answering these questions may take some time, but what you gain from each evaluation will improve your evaluating skills and increase your confidence in your skills. A lack of confidence and courage will cause you to miss out on some opportunities that could have helped you meet or exceed your goals.

EXERCISE NO. 8

Developing Your Investment Insight

Read any newspaper or magazine article and answer the following questions about the article:

a. How can someone make money now with this information?
b. How can someone position himself or herself to make money in the future with this information?
c. Who (a type of existing company or a type of person) can make money now with this information?
d. Who (a type of existing company or a type of person) will be hurt by not having this information?

Doing this exercise regularly will help develop your ability to recognize potential opportunities and keep your insights fresh.

KEY POINTS

To make money through your investments, you need to find "Gooses" with the golden eggs. Getting only golden eggs will just give you money to spend. Truly great investors find the "Gooses" that provide a constant supply of golden eggs.

To develop your insights and your ability to recognize potential opportunities, you can evaluate potential opportunities by asking questions in six categories: pre-evaluation, opportunity and industry, comparing the numbers, evaluating growth potential, developing your insight, and determining whether the opportunity is a potential goose with golden eggs.

STEP NINE

Staying Focused

Overcoming Distractions and Remaining Focused on Wealth Mentality Thoughts and Actions

Free flowing success and passion comes from identifying that "well" which flows deepest and greatest within you. Most people continue to tap into their shallow "wells" and never grow to peak performance.
      Dr. Jeffrey Magee, author of *Yield Management*

The ability to remain focused and not allow yourself to be distracted is one of the most overlooked and underdeveloped skills necessary to achieve your goals.

I know that at the start of your journey, the discipline required to remain focused on *Wealth Mentality Thoughts* and *Actions* can be difficult to keep up given the pressures and temptations presented in everyday life. So this ninth step includes seven things you can do to stay focused. They are: make a commitment, compose a wealth development philosophy, write a mission statement, use positive affirmations, practice visualization, use reminders, make your own motivational tape, and learn to relax.

Make a Commitment

One of the most powerful things you can do to direct thoughts is to make a commitment. Making a commitment to something gives you direction and something to focus on.

Think about it. What took place the last time you accomplished something that really felt good? Did it just happen without any pre-work?

More than likely, this great accomplishment took place because you made a commitment to accomplish something in particular at some point in the past. You planned, thought about it, took the steps to get to your destination, and took the action to make your success happen.

Unless you make a complete commitment to the goals you set, your chances of focusing on and reaching those goals will remain small.

Compose a Wealth Development Philosophy

If you asked most people to state their philosophy of life, they would probably say that they have no specific philosophy. This answer would be wrong in most cases. Whether you know it or not, most of your thoughts and actions come from a specific philosophy, formed after years and years of experiences and testing thoughts and beliefs. This philosophy is a part of the thought and belief systems to which you align your lifestyle.

For example, when your philosophy says that wealth is a real possibility, that idea will make its way into your thoughts. If reinforced, you will come to believe it is true. From this philosophy will flow all thoughts and beliefs that have to do with money, happiness, and providing for your family and yourself. Once this happens, you will find yourself adjusting your motivation, wants, needs, environment and behavior to the thought that wealth is a real possibility.

Composing and reinforcing your own specific philosophy regarding wealth development will go a long way in helping you to stay focused on *Wealth Mentality Thoughts* and *Actions*. I recommend that you keep it short so that you memorize and repeat it to yourself daily and as often as needed. The philosophy should include some aspect of pursuing, attaining, maintaining, and growing wealth.

For example, my wealth development philosophy can be summed in four words: GET THE "GOOSES" FIRST. It states:

> Because I have *Wealth Mentality*, I value and acquire the "Gooses" first so that I will always have golden eggs. I need only one goose, but it is better to have as many as I am capable of nurturing.

Write a Mission Statement

Why are you here? What are your objectives in life? What kind of person do you want to be? How would you like to be described after your earthly body has expired? The answers to these and other questions are all part of a mission statement. A mission statement describes the reason you do what you do and why you attempt to be who and what you are.

A philosophy has more to do with your basic values, while a mission statement concentrates on your actions. For instance, my mission statement for this book and myself states:

> My mission as an author and educator is to use my knowledge and talents to help others discover a *Wealth Mentality* within them so that they can live more prosperous and more fulfilled lives.

Use Positive Affirmations

An affirmation is a statement that establishes as true a belief you want to plant in your subconscious mind. Positive affirmations are statements that focus on what you want to accomplish, not on what you don't want to accomplish. The idea is that when you say the same things to yourself over and over again, you will begin to believe them. If you believe them, you will do the things that will turn the statements into reality.

To some, this may sound a little "12-steppish," but "12-step" programs can work. I can tell you that affirmations do work for me. Remember when I talked about *thought barriers?* Positive Affirmations are a way to overcome your *thought barriers* and move your wealth plan forward because they use your words to help you create a vision of what you can accomplish. Your words can be a source of encouragement and comfort if you allow them to be. Positive affirmations are easy to use when you are in a time crunch.

A few examples of affirmations regarding wealth building are:

- I am wealthy.
- I deserve wealth in my life.
- I am a savvy businessperson.
- I have a great eye for asset building opportunities.
- Money is a tool that I use well.
- Wealth is attracted to me.
- I recognize opportunities to build wealth in all things.
- I take action.
- I am an active and successful player in the wealth building game.

Here are a few guidelines to create your own positive affirmations:

- Make it easy to remember.

- Try to keep it brief. This is helpful at the beginning of your process until you get used to using affirmations. However, you can make it as long as you want. The key is to be able to remember it.

- Keep it positive by focusing on what you want, not what you don't want.

- Select words that evoke an emotional response within you.
- Keep it in the present tense.

Positive affirmations should be repeated no less than five times in a row in the morning, the afternoon and before you go to sleep.

Practice Visualization

We all create images in our minds that are with us all the time. From wishful thinking to monsters in the closet to how we view ourselves in relation to the world, the images we create are sometimes so powerful that we believe we "see" things that aren't there. We allow these images to influence our thoughts and ultimately our behavior. That is the power of visualization; allowing your behavior to be influenced by the pictures in your mind. Visualization can be a powerful tool in developing and maintaining a *Wealth Mentality*.

Having negative images about your ability or worthiness to achieve wealth leads to negative attitudes and behaviors regarding wealth development. Your behavior will support your negative attitudes whether your attitudes are conscious or sub-conscious. Then, the results of your negative behavior reinforce your negative attitudes, which in turn reinforce your negative behavior. This negative cycle will continue until you choose to break it.

I find that visualization exercises work best for me directly following a positive affirmation session. To be most effective, your mental images must be detailed. They should involve all the senses by including sights, sounds, smells, temperature, your thoughts, emotions, actions, and others' reactions to you. Like positive affirmations, I recommend visualization exercises three times a day, preferably following your positive affirmation exercises. To get started, visualize the following scenarios:

- Visualize yourself accomplishing your wealth goals.

- Visualize yourself efficiently doing and completing productive tasks in the morning.

- Visualize yourself efficiently doing and completing productive tasks in the afternoon.

- Visualize yourself efficiently doing and completing productive tasks in the evening.

- Visualize yourself getting peaceful rest and dreaming of positive ways to respond to situations you're dealing with.

Remember, you will become better at visualizations over time.

Use Reminders

Sometimes you just need a little inspiration or to be reminded of what you're doing and why you're doing it to get you back on track. Items such as post-its, posters or plaques throughout your home, on your desk at work, or any other place where you spend a lot of time can cue your thoughts back to focusing on the task at hand. These reminders can contain any message you like, such as inspirational quotes, your goals for the day, your long-term goals, or your mission statement. They can be homemade, like the collage I mentioned in Step Seven, or purchased retail.

Make Your Own Motivational Tape

One of my favorite things to do is to record my own motivational tape or CD. These tapes contain my life philosophies, my mission statement, affirmations, and inspirational stories and quotes. These things are mixed-in between songs with lyrics that always uplift me. I play them wherever and whenever I need encouragement.

You can make tapes to encourage you in specific situations, such as when you are disappointed, when you don't feel that you're getting any results from your efforts, and when you've experienced a setback.

Learn to Relax

Being in a relaxed state helps clear away the mental clutter so that you can think with clarity about information you have received. Thinking with clarity is essential to making intelligent and informed decisions.

There are many ways to relax. The following are several ways that work for me.

- **Exercise**

Once you get into it, there is nothing like exercising to relax your mind. The hardest part of exercising is getting started. However, once your program is in full-gear, you will begin to see exercise as a way to focus your mind and improve the condition of your body at the same time. I am always amazed at how much energy I have after a workout. I always wish that I had started sooner. I am sure those who exercise regularly can relate to the "I can conquer the world" feeling you have after a workout. A relaxed mind and an energized spirit can accomplish much.

- **Meditation**

When I begin to feel overwhelmed by a situation, I take a moment to meditate. Meditation provides the conditions that allow me to explore my deepest intuition and levels of creativity. While meditating, I leave all thoughts of the situation behind for awhile. I immerse myself in the sounds and images that amplify and encourage my inner purpose, values and desires. It is somewhere in the stillness of silent reflection that my answers are illuminated. It never fails me.

- **Start a hobby**

If you are looking for something to totally take your mind off your day or situation, start doing something that produces tangible results. Gardening accomplishes this for me. I have found it impossible to be concerned with *any* cares of life while gardening. I can stay for hours in the garden without realizing how much time has passed. The feelings of pride and accomplishment I get from creating something of such beauty, usually from nothing, fuels my confidence so that I can achieve other goals.

- **Get in touch with nature**

Allow yourself to use all of your senses and become immersed in nature. Take the time to "smell the roses," literally and figuratively. Plant a garden, go on nature walks, bird watching, or learn how to arrange flowers. The awesomeness of nature will inspire, uplift, and keep you centered. You will learn to appreciate that you are a part of something greater than yourself.

- **Explore your inner artist**

Whether it is watching a play or acting in a play, going to a museum or taking a painting or sculpturing class, allow yourself to explore any artistic interest or ability you have. Perhaps you enjoy writing. Start writing poetry or keeping a journal of your thoughts, visions, dreams, actions, or positive statements that you hear throughout the day.

- **Talk with friends**

Take a break and make a phone call to a close friend. Friends are the best people for relaxing with because they ask nothing of you but friendship. I hope you have at least one close friend on whom you can rely to help regenerate your heart, mind, and soul.

- **Take a short nap in the afternoon (make sure it's short!)**

I'm sure some of you may be laughing right now! I am a great believer in the power of "Power Naps." They really work! It is a practice that has been used in Europe for hundreds of years. Europeans and other cultures take a short *siesta* after lunch, which revitalizes them each afternoon. There have been many studies on the beneficial effects of napping in the middle of your day. How short should your nap be? As long as it takes to refresh yourself without making you groggy. Thomas Edison used to lie down on his couch while holding a handful of marbles. He would hang his hand with the marbles off the couch, just above a tin plate. When Edison fell into a deep sleep, the marbles would fall from his hand into the tin plate. This made such a noise that Edison would wake up. The great inventor said this process awakened him during his "creative" sleep phase and left him more alert, creative and refreshed.

- **Take a walk alone or with others**

You don't have to take a nature walk. You can just walk through your neighborhood, down the street, or in the building where you work. If you're walking alone, use the time to let your mind go blank before pondering any thoughts. When the thoughts come, guide them toward relaxation. Do not let them stress you. If the thoughts that come are stressful, use the positive affirmations I spoke of earlier.

- **Make a hot cup of tea**

The Eastern sages have been publicizing the relaxing power of tea for thousands of years. I am such a believer in the relaxing effect of teas that I have developed and produced my own line of them! Here are a few quick tips for you to get the best use out of a cup of tea. Start with very cold water instead of warm or hot water. Cold water has more oxygen, which adds to the flavor of the tea. Make sure the tea you use is aromatic and leave the bag in long enough to give the liquid real flavor (at least 1-3 minutes). Try to drink it while it is still as hot as you are comfortable with. The warmth will carry through your system and fill you with a relaxed disposition. While drinking the tea, look at or visualize a serene setting. I'm feeling relaxed just thinking about it!

 # EXERCISE NO. 9

Staying Focused

Pick one of the focus methods to start implementing now. Try a new method each week. For example, if you choose to start with writing your mission statement, stay with that task until your statement is completed. Repeat the statement no less than five times a day as well as during times when you notice that you're being distracted. You'll find that it won't be long before you've memorized the statement and won't need to refer to your notes.

By learning how to use each of the focus methods in this step, you will have the tools needed to redirect your thoughts when they stray.

KEY POINTS

The discipline of staying focused is among the most important things you can learn in developing your *Wealth Mentality*. There are many things you can do to help yourself stay focused:

- Make a commitment
- Compose a wealth development philosophy
- Write a mission statement
- Use positive affirmations
- Practice visualization
- Use reminders
- Make your own motivational tape
- Learn to relax

There are many ways to relax. Among those I suggest are:

- Exercising
- Meditating
- Starting a hobby
- Getting in touch with nature
- Exploring your inner artist
- Talking with friends
- Taking a short nap
- Taking a walk
- Making a hot cup of tea

PHASE THREE

Maintaining Your Wealth Mentality

STEP TEN

Developing Wealth Mentality Habits
Keeping and Building Upon Wealth Mentality Thoughts and Actions

The individual who wants to reach the top in business must appreciate the might of the force of habit and must understand that practices are what create habits. He must be quick to break those habits that can break him and hasten to adopt those practices that will become the habits that help him achieve the success he desires.
        J. Paul Getty, American Oil Tycoon

Now that you've learned what thoughts and actions it takes to develop a *Wealth Mentality*, learning what it takes to maintain it is the next order of business. Your ability to maintain a *Wealth Mentality* will depend upon whether or not you are able to turn the thoughts and actions you took to get a *Wealth Mentality* into habits.

In this step, I'll discuss what habits are, why we develop them, and how to get rid of the unwanted ones. Developing wealth building habits is not only the key to maintaining a *Wealth Mentality* and achieving wealth, but also to having a well-rounded and fulfilling life.

What Are Habits?

A habit is a behavior pattern that seems to be involuntary after many repetitions. In other words, a habit is doing something over and over until it becomes an automatic process. A habit can be anything from sitting in the same seat on the train each day to sleeping until the last minute in the morning.

Doing things habitually, *i.e.*, automatically, frees your conscious thinking to focus on more productive matters. Productive habits are key to having and maintaining a *Wealth Mentality*. Having productive habits is like having your own personal auto pilot that you never turn off. Your auto pilot is constantly guiding you toward your intended destination even when you are not at the controls. For example, some people may think having a *Wealth Mentality* means that they will be consumed with thoughts of making money. They picture themselves trapped in their home or office, with no social life and no friends, obsessing over money. **THEY COULDN'T BE MORE WRONG.**

If you are able to turn your *Wealth Mentality Thoughts* and *Actions* into habits, you won't have to be consumed with thoughts of making money or be worried about having enough money because your auto pilot constantly keeps in motion the actions necessary to secure your future wealth. With your conscious mind free to pursue other interests, you can have a well rounded and fulfilling life.

Why Do We Develop Habits?

Most habits have a positive origin. They developed for a good reason — to help or protect you in some way. However, once the need for the habit is gone, the habit tends to remain and grow stronger, sometimes to a fault.

Howard had a habit of keeping his desk so clean that he could see his reflection. He developed this habit 45 years ago, when his first boss told him that "a clean desk is the sign of a clear mind."

Every day, at the end of the day, Howard would put everything away, brush off any small papers that remained and shined the desk so that it would be spotless. Never mind that the cleaning crew would probably do the same later. Howard believed that you could never shine the desk often enough.

Howard climbed the corporate ladder and after 45 years of a highly successful career, he retired. He went home to be with his wife full-time. Within a week, she found him shining the counters and the furniture one or two times a day. Within three months, Howard was up to polishing practically all of the furniture in the house three and four times a day. With less to do, Howard increased the times he took to his habit — and drove his wife crazy!

Howard needed to able to separate work from home and recognize that his perceived need to have a clear mind by keeping a clean desk ended when he retired. Even though the need ended, Howard's habit escalated to become a compulsion for him and a source of frustration for his wife.

How do you know if a habit is negative or has the potential to become negative? Examine the consequences of the habit in question. If the consequences are harmful to you or others, then it is a bad habit and you should consider getting rid of it.

How Do We Get Rid of Unwanted Habits?

Unwanted habits generally won't go away just because you want them to. Habits develop with the intention of helping you in some way. They serve to fulfill your needs. Your subconscious mind will not allow you simply to abandon an unwanted habit because you would be left unprotected, or your need will go unsatisfied.

The subconscious mind doesn't care how the need is satisfied so long as it is satisfied. If you need to relax, your subconscious will seek to make you feel relaxed. It doesn't care if you smoke, take tranquilizers, read, or exercise, so long as you relax. This is where you must use your conscious mind to fulfill the need to relax with something that is not self-destructive.

In Howard's case, after having polished every piece of furniture in the house several times, he could have realized that he enjoyed making furniture look clean and new. Perhaps instead of polishing his own furniture, he could have started restoring antique furniture as hobby. (Hopefully, Howard had some available space in his garage or basement so that his new hobby would not become a new source of frustration for his wife.) Perhaps, if thinking and acting with a *Wealth Mentality*, Howard could have started an antique furniture restoration business and earned money while doing something he enjoyed. Or, Howard could simply have gotten out of the house and taken up golf.

Remember what I said earlier: you are in control of your actions. The key to replacing an unwanted habit with a productive one is to determine the need that the habit is attempting to fulfill. Once you determine the need, *find positive ways to satisfy the need.* I know this sounds too simple, but simplicity is its beauty and the key to its effectiveness.

EXERCISE NO. 10

Overcoming Habits that Block Wealth

a. Make a list of the habits that have kept you from developing wealth. Because habits are actions you take on a regular basis without consciously thinking about them, you will have to work to become more aware of your behavior. Ask those close to you for their opinions on any wealth blocking habits they have observed in you.
b. Go through the list and describe the benefit you get from each habit.
c. What reasons do you give yourself for continuing to do the habit?
d. Can you visualize being satisfied without the habit?
e. How can you get the benefits of the habit without keeping the habit?

By getting rid of habits that block wealth, and turning *Wealth Mentality Thoughts* and *Actions* into productive habits, you can put your wealth building efforts on auto pilot.

KEY POINTS

Maintaining a *Wealth Mentality* requires that you turn *Wealth Mentality Thoughts* and *Actions* into habits. Habits are behavior patterns that become automatic as a result of your having done them over and over. It's like having your own auto pilot. When wealth building becomes a habit, you don't have to spend every waking moment thinking about your wealth goals because they are being taken care of automatically. Your conscious mind will be free to pursue other interests.

Your habits develop to help or protect you. Despite good intentions, the effects of some habits can be self-destructive. You must examine the effects of your habits and get rid of the ones that prevent you getting the things you want. It will be necessary to explore your deepest thoughts to determine the need the habit is trying to satisfy, and then find positive ways to satisfy it.

STEP ELEVEN

Dealing with Setbacks
Going From Disappointments to Accomplishments

A setback is never the end of the road. It is a bend in the road. The only ones who crash or go broke are those who fail to turn, to change, to stretch, and try new ways to get to their goals.

Willie Jolley, author of
A Setback is a Setup for a Comeback

Aah! So you've done or have prepared to do all the things I suggested you do to develop and maintain a *Wealth Mentality*. Then, something happens in the world that changes everything — an oil crisis, a terrorist attack, a large and well-known company lays off thousands of workers and creates a crisis of confidence in world markets. Your investments lose their value, you may lose your job, interest rates are cut and the return on your T-bills falls, and suddenly you don't feel so confident anymore.

Can this happen? You bet it can.

Setbacks happen often and in everything you do. So much of life is two steps forward, one step back, three steps forward, two steps back, one step forward, two steps back, five steps forward, three steps back.

Let's see ... if you add that up, you're still three steps ahead of where you started.

Dealing with Setbacks

If you're going to go for wealth, you must be prepared for things not to go the way you want them to, *i.e.*, you must be prepared to deal with setbacks. The key to dealing with setbacks is to respond to them immediately and in the appropriate way. If you recognize that setbacks can be a launching pad for even greater opportunities, then setbacks will just be temporary.

So, here are ten *Wealth Mentality Thoughts* for dealing with setbacks.

1. A *Wealth Mentality* thinks "Patience"

A *Wealth Mentality* knows that it may take some time for the desired behavior to become part of a routine. Therefore, a *Wealth Mentality* is not afraid or discouraged by setbacks.

2. A *Wealth Mentality* thinks "Inevitability"

A *Wealth Mentality* knows that setbacks are inevitable. Since you don't have a crystal ball and can't predict the future with 100% accuracy, mistakes and bad judgments will happen. Therefore a *Wealth Mentality* is prepared for setbacks.

In September 1991, AT&T had every reason to believe that it had scored a coup in the exploding information distribution market. It had just purchased NCR, which AT&T saw as the computer powerhouse that would give it a dominant role in that arena. At the time, AT&T Chairman Robert Allen bragged that the $7.5 billion takeover would "link people, organizations and their information in a seamless global computer network."

It didn't turn out that way. The renamed AT&T Global Information Systems found itself with "plunging profits and stalled sales." In 1995, AT&T GIS lost more than $325 million. In spinning off the division, AT&T took a 1.6 billion dollar charge off against earnings to cover its costs.

In 1996, Quaker Oats paid $1.7 billion for the soaring cult drink favorite Snapple. It seemed a perfect fit. Two years later, it unloaded the drink company for $300 million, one-sixth of what it had paid. During its two years of ownership, the bottom fell out of the boutique juice market and sales dropped by more than 35% — from 70 million cases to 45 million. Eventually, the purchase was a cited factor in Quaker Oats president William Smithberg losing his job and making the company itself a takeover target.

The company that purchased Snapple from Quaker stopped the free fall, flattened out the sales, and eventually turned the numbers in a positive direction.

Setbacks will happen. Things won't always turn out the way you expect.

3. A *Wealth Mentality* thinks "Solution"

A *Wealth Mentality* knows that it is useless to fret or wallow over disappointments or setbacks. Therefore, when they happen, a *Wealth Mentality* immediately seeks a "temporary solution" to keep things on track. A *Wealth Mentality* then takes the time to investigate why the situation occurred and evaluate ways to prevent or minimize the chances of the situation happening again. It may be that a bunch of mini-decisions led to the setback or it may have been one big one (It is usually a bunch of mini-ones). It is after obtaining all available information that a *Wealth Mentality* puts a more permanent solution in place.

4. A *Wealth Mentality* thinks "Steadfast"

A *Wealth Mentality* knows that remaining on the path to wealth is not easy. Temptations and distractions are around every corner looking to take you on a detour. The path to wealth is not straight. It is a winding path that sometimes seems to go in circles. But remaining steadfast to the course eventually gets you where you want to go.

5. A *Wealth Mentality* thinks "Lessons"

A *Wealth Mentality* knows that learning by trial and error, the way most people learn, usually wastes time. Therefore, a *Wealth Mentality* seeks to learn lessons based on other people's experiences. Don't try to reinvent the wheel when you don't have to. You can achieve your goals more quickly by learning to build on others' successes and avoiding their mistakes. Seek out more information and guidance and keep updating the information. Having inaccurate or outdated information leads to misguided strategies and causes setbacks.

6. A *Wealth Mentality* thinks "Overestimate"

A *Wealth Mentality* knows that it is common to miscalculate what it will take to achieve any goal. Therefore a *Wealth Mentality* expects that it will require at least twice what is believed necessary to achieve its wealth goals. Failing to budget enough time, energy, and money to achieve your goals leads to half-done efforts. Half-done efforts lead to setbacks.

7. A *Wealth Mentality* thinks "Self-Control"

A *Wealth Mentality* knows that, while emotions are necessary, allowing emotions to be the driving force of your behavior is a recipe for disappointment and setbacks. Therefore, a *Wealth Mentality* keeps emotions in check.

8. A *Wealth Mentality* thinks "Self-Respect"

A *Wealth Mentality* knows that what you say to yourself is ultimately more important than what others say to you. Therefore, a *Wealth Mentality* keeps self-talk in check. Make sure the things you are saying to yourself are geared toward moving forward, not moving backward. Make sure the statements you're making are positive and valid.

9. A *Wealth Mentality* thinks "Simplicity"

A *Wealth Mentality* knows that the simplest solution is usually the best solution. Therefore, a *Wealth Mentality* doesn't disregard possible solutions just because of their simplicity. I have seen many ideas, including the idea of needing a *Wealth Mentality*, dismissed just because they *seem* too simple. Give all possible solutions a try, especially the simple ones.

10. A *Wealth Mentality* thinks "Opportunity"

A *Wealth Mentality* knows that setbacks can be a launching pad for an even greater opportunity. Therefore, a *Wealth Mentality* proactively seeks out the opportunity in every seemingly bad or frustrating situation. In the midst of a situation, ask yourself, "What can I learn from this?" or "How can I use this situation to work for me?"

Review Step Ten for ways to stay focused on these thoughts when you experience setbacks, so that your setbacks are only temporary. Remember, the history of financial success is littered with the stories of those who found their true calling and true wealth when they lost the job or relationship they thought would be theirs forever. Disappointment and failure forces you to regroup and look at things in a different way. The question is: Will you let setbacks get you down, or will you use them to catapult you to greater successes than you've ever imagined? Allow the thoughts from this step to help you regroup.

EXERCISE NO. 11

Logging Your Setbacks

a. Create a log for future setbacks. First, write down the setback. Include a section for what caused the setback, how it specifically affected your pursuit of wealth, and how you plan to overcome it. Be as detailed as possible.
b. Start the log by writing about past setbacks, what caused them, how they affected your pursuit of wealth, and how you overcame them.

By keeping a log of your setbacks, you can begin to uncover possible patterns to your behavior and setbacks. You can use this information to prevent certain setbacks from happening in the future.

KEY POINTS

Setbacks are inevitable. Therefore, you must deal with setbacks swiftly and effectively. When experiencing a setback, a *Wealth Mentality* thinks:

- "Patience"
- "Inevitability"
- "Solution"
- "Steadfast"
- "Lessons"
- "Overestimate"
- "Self-Control"
- "Self-Respect"
- "Simplicity"
- "Opportunity"

Focusing on these thoughts will help direct your thinking toward solutions and help you capitalize on setbacks.

---

www.wealthmentality.com

PHASE FOUR

Developing Your Wealth Action Plan

STEP TWELVE

Problems with Wealth Action Plans
Avoiding Two of the Most Overlooked Problems with Wealth Action Plans

Learn from the mistakes of others. You won't live long enough to make them all yourself.

Unknown

We've come to the point in this process where you should now be ready to start thinking about your *Wealth Action Plan*.

If you've thought long and hard about the things I've told you, and then actually did the things I've talked about, you should be well on your way in your *Wealth Mentality* journey. Now you can really start thinking about what you need to do to acquire wealth and keep that wealth coming.

It is often said that what you don't know can't hurt you. I don't believe that the people who say that are wealthy. What you don't know can hurt you. In fact, what you don't know can cause you devastation beyond imagination and knock you down to financial ground zero. Therefore, when I teach somebody how to do something, I usually find it effective to first uncover the possible problems (*i.e.*, things they may not know) they can experience in the process, determine how they can avoid them, and then start the process.

So the first thing I want to talk about in this phase are two of the most common problems you may encounter when putting together your *Wealth Action Plan*.

Problem #1

A common problem with *Wealth Action Plans* is that the model used to come up with the plan is *wrong*. The *wrong* model to achieve wealth looks like this:

SUCCESS	=	WEALTH
Success at something that produces high earned income.		A condition in which: (1) you live in abundance such that you do not have to choose between needs and wants, (2) you don't need earned income to maintain abundance, and (3) you are at peace with yourself financially.

For many people, success is working hard in a high-income profession and being the best at what they do. They believe that being successful in this way will make them wealthy. This is one of the reasons there is what is called a "rat race" and why millions of people are discouraged by their current financial positions despite having a high earned income.

As many have discovered, simply making more money does not automatically lead you to wealth. It is what you *do* with the money *you have* that enables you to satisfy condition number "(2)" from the wealth definition above, *i.e.*, acquire the assets that allow you to maintain your condition of abundance without having to physically

www.wealthmentality.com

work to earn an income. That is where a *Wealth Mentality* comes in. A *Wealth Mentality* is the missing ingredient in most plans to achieve wealth.

Compare the model above to this model:

SUCCESS	+	WEALTH MENTALITY	=	WEALTH
Success at something that produces high earned income.		A mind programmed to recognize and compel you to take advantage of wealth opportunities (i.e., to put your earned income to work for you), thus producing passive income (*MADE Money*).		A condition in which: (1) you live in abundance such that you do not have to choose between needs and wants, (2) you don't need earned income to maintain abundance, and (3) you are at peace with yourself financially.

Having read this far, does this model make more sense to you? Only when you introduce a *Wealth Mentality* into the equation can you arrive at a place in which (1) you live in a condition of abundance such that you do not have to choose between needs and wants; (2) you don't need earned income to maintain your condition of abundance; and (3) you are at peace with yourself financially. Then, and only then, can you truly say you are wealthy.

Therefore, make sure that your *Wealth Action Plan* contains elements that help you continue to develop and maintain a *Wealth Mentality*, with a particular emphasis on managing the influences on your thoughts that I discussed in Step Four (physical condition, beliefs, values, desires, needs and environment).

www.wealthmentality.com

Problem #2

Another common problem is that most *Wealth Action Plans* do not address *personal goals* as a whole. It is possible for a plan focused exclusively on the material aspects of wealth to make you wealthy, but it can leave you unsatisfied with your life as a whole. Remember, wealth is only a tool to help you get more enjoyment out of the other areas of your life. If you are not getting enjoyment out of the other areas of your life, you may lose the motivation to stay on your *Wealth Action Plan*.

 EXERCISE NO. 12

What are Your Nonmaterial Goals?

Assume you inherited $5 million.

a. List the first five things that you would do with the money. Are any of the five things fulfilling a nonmaterial goal?
b. If you had to give all the money away to a charity or other worthwhile causes for which you would receive no tangible benefits, to whom or what would you give the money? Why?

Identifying and incorporating your nonmaterial goals into your *Wealth Action Plan* will keep you balanced, give you an overall feeling of satisfaction, and help you enjoy the wealth you achieve.

KEY POINTS

It is important to know about the problems you can encounter in developing your own *Wealth Action Plan* so that you can find ways to try and avoid the problems and achieve your goals more quickly.

Make sure that your *Wealth Action Plan* includes elements that help you develop and maintain a *Wealth Mentality* and fulfill personal goals. As you continue to develop and maintain your *Wealth Mentality*, you will continue to recognize and take advantage of more wealth building opportunities. And as you witness how having wealth helps you fulfill your personal goals, you will become more motivated to continue to achieve your wealth goals.

STEP THIRTEEN
How Much is Wealth to You?
Establishing Actual Numbers for Your Wealth Vision

Money is a sixth sense, which makes it possible for us to enjoy the other five.

Richard Ney, American writer

In 1999, Roy and Linda Greenberg were — by any comparison to nationwide statistics — doing quite well. With both spouses working in professional positions, their combined income came in just over $100,000. They had just gotten an offer for their suburban, split-level, three-bedroom home. The offer was a whopping $285,000.

The national statistics showed that the median income for married couples that year was $56,800, and the average home price was around $115,000. Comparing their numbers to averages, this couple was rolling in the money. Except for one thing — Roy and Linda lived in Westchester County, New York, which had one of the highest costs of living in the United States.

Roy and Linda wanted to "upgrade" from their house to a slightly larger house in a better school district. They felt that in order to provide the best for their family, they needed to find better schools, safer streets, and a different environment.

They eventually found the kind of house they were looking for, paying $415,000 and driving their yearly property tax bill from $7,500 to $12,000. Talking to friends after buying the house, they said with great resignation, "If somebody had told me 15 years ago that I would be making six figures and struggling financially, I'd have laughed at them."

At the same time, one of their neighbors, Arlene DeRosa, found out her job was being transferred to a suburb of Atlanta, Georgia. Arlene and her husband, Jim, put their split-level, 1,800 sq. ft., three-bedroom house on the market and sold it for the same $285,000. They moved to the Atlanta suburbs, where they bought a 4,200-sq. ft. colonial, five-bedroom house with a finished basement. The area had better schools and a better environment for their family. They paid $285,000 for the Atlanta house, while dropping their yearly property tax bill to $2,900.

Getting into bed that night, Arlene turned to Jim and said, "In Westchester, we were middle-class. Here, we're wealthy."

Which couple is wealthier?

Like success, every person has his or her own definition of "how much" is wealth. Wealth is relative and theoretical. While most of the world quantifies wealth by possessions, wealth is also an experience for the individual. That is why there is no one right answer to the question "Which couple is wealthier?" That is also why my earlier definition of wealth contains an element of personal feelings. To restate, you are wealthy when, at the very least:

1. You live in a condition of abundance such that you don't have to choose between providing for you or your family's needs and wants and pursuing your dreams.

2. You don't need <u>earned</u> income (*i.e.*, you don't need to work) to maintain your condition of abundance, <u>and</u>

3. You are at peace with yourself financially.

This definition contains both objective and subjective elements. What doesn't this definition contain? It doesn't contain an actual dollar amount. That's the subjective part. As I'll discuss below, the actual dollar amount is for you to decide. Let's take a look at these three elements of wealth.

- **You live in a condition of abundance such that you don't have to choose between providing for you or your family's needs and wants and pursuing your dreams.**

The condition of abundance to which I'm referring is when you have more than enough to take care of your needs and wants, your family's needs and wants *and* be able to pursue your dreams. This element of wealth is satisfied when what you do with your time and money are not decisions based purely on the availability of money.

For example, it has been your dream to take your family to tour Italy, your parents' homeland. You book the trip and make preparations to go. One week before you're scheduled to leave, you find out that your daughter needs braces. You also find out that your son's school band will be marching in the annual Rose Bowl parade, which takes place out-of-state. You must pay for his costs to participate within the next two months. To top it off, last night's windstorm severely damaged your home's roof and it requires immediate repair. Do you still go on the trip to Italy? You may decide to stay because you want to supervise the roof repair. However, to satisfy the "condition of abundance" component of wealth, your decision of whether to still go to Italy can't be based on whether you have enough money to pay for the braces, the Rose Bowl trip, the new roof, and the trip to Italy. When you're wealthy, you have enough to do all of those things and not have to sell an asset or alter your lifestyle one bit.

- **You don't need earned income to maintain your condition of abundance.**

To satisfy this component of wealth, you must not require a paycheck to maintain your condition of abundance. You may choose to work for a variety of reasons unrelated to "needing" the money. In the example above, your paycheck must not be needed to cover the braces, the Rose Bowl trip, the new roof, the trip to Italy, and your continued everyday living expenses. The income your assets produce must be sufficient to pay for all of your lifestyle expenses.

- **You are at peace with yourself financially.**

I know that some people believe that whether or not you are wealthy in a financial sense has nothing to do with how you feel personally. Many of these people believe that you are wealthy only if you have a net worth of least one million dollars. If you believe this as well, and you want to be wealthy, then you will not be at peace with yourself financially until you have a net worth of at least one million dollars.

I do not believe that anyone can or should dictate an actual amount of net worth for you to seek. Just make sure that the amount you choose satisfies the three conditions above. Otherwise, it doesn't matter what the rest of the world thinks. As I said earlier, wealth is relative and personal. Someone who comes from a poverty background may require less (or quite possibly more) than a million-dollar net worth to be at peace with himself financially. Someone who comes from a wealthy background may need to achieve a substantially higher net worth to feel at peace. Conversely, if you grew up with wealth, you may not even need a million dollar net worth to feel at peace with yourself financially.

How much does it take for you to live in a condition of abundance? How much income do your assets have to produce every month to maintain your condition of abundance? How much do you need to be at peace with yourself financially?

Your answers to the questions above depend on your view of the world and your view of your place in this world. We've all known people who hold down two or three jobs in order to make ends meet; people who see wealth as having a big car, bigger house and other status symbols their neighbors could envy. And we've also known people who choose to leave the corporate rat race to stay home and take care of their kids; open a small business; or do more volunteer work, knowing they will be making less money.

Part of having a *Wealth Mentality* is having a clear and specific vision of where you want to be financially, and when you want to be there. Your vision provides the framework within which you choose your financial goals. Your goals are a direct by-product of the vision you actually have for your future. If the vision is weak, then the goals will not have the mental support needed to achieve them. Providing the mental support needed to achieve your goals is the purpose and very essence of a *Wealth Mentality*.

EXERCISE NO. 13

How Much Do You Want?

Picture yourself as you want to be and the environment you want be in 2, 5, 10, and 20 years from now.

a. Write down the things you see, the things you've accomplished, and the situations you're in.
b. For each item, goal, and situation on your list, estimate how much you think you would have had to earn to have those things, achieve those goals and be in those situations.
c. Do some research to confirm your estimates and modify them as necessary.
d. What's the total? This is a number that you can start to work with. Naturally, the number will change as you receive more information.

By coming up with an actual dollar amount of wealth to pursue, you are giving your mind something concrete on which to focus and organize your behavior around.

KEY POINTS

Being wealthy means that you live in a condition of abundance, you don't need a paycheck to maintain your abundance, and that you are at peace with yourself financially. What constitutes abundance for you, and exactly how much you need to be at peace with yourself are things that only you can decide.

You must have a clear and specific vision of your financial future. Having a clear and specific vision helps you select goals that actually accomplishes your vision and provides the mental support you need to achieve your goals.

STEP FOURTEEN

Where Are You Now, Financially?

Assessing Your Current Financial Position So That You Can Direct Your Progress

Why is there so much month left at the end of the money?
John Barrymore, American actor

Now that you have a vision of where you want your journey to take you, you still need to determine your starting point before you can develop a plan to get there.

Part of a *Wealth Mentality* is knowing your current financial picture and, ultimately, having a game plan to address and manage each of the following parts of your financial picture:

- Spending Habits
- Emergency Funds
- Insurance Needs
- Investments
- Estate Planning
- Savings
- Bad Debt
- Taxes
- Retirement

Step Fifteen will address how to use these areas to build a brighter financial picture for yourself and your family. To get to that point, start with your current financial picture.

There are two documents that you must understand how to prepare and use in order to know where you stand financially: an *income statement* and a *balance sheet*. An income statement shows how much income flows in and out of your life during a certain time period. A balance sheet shows how well you have put your income to work for you at a particular point in time.

Periodic examinations of your income statement and balance sheet will help you determine your areas of strength and weakness, manage your money more effectively, set and prioritize goals, and monitor your progress. Having this information readily available will also help you communicate more effectively with a professional advisor if you decide to use one.

The next two forms will help you prepare an income statement and balance sheet. They will take some work and require you to get information from many sources. If you don't want to write in this book, you can obtain blank income statement and balance sheet forms from this book's web site. Don't cheat yourself by skipping these exercises.

EXERCISE NO. 14a

Prepare Your Income Statement

	Average for Month	Total for Year
INCOME		
Earned Income (Your Pay Check)		
Bonuses		
Income from Investments (Interest, Rental Income, Dividends, etc.)		
Other Income (Alimony, Child Support, etc.)		
Total Income: $		
EXPENSES	How much is interest monthly?	
Mortgage or Rent*		
Car Loan Payment*		
Credit Card Payments*		
Loan Payments (Investments, etc.)*		
Total of Monthly Interest	$	
Property Taxes		
Other Taxes Not Withheld		
Food		
Utilities		
Insurance Premiums (Car, Life, Health, etc.)		
Commuting Expenses (Gas, Bus/Train Pass)		
Medical Expenses (not covered by insurance)		
Clothing and Personal Care		
Charitable Contributions		
Recreation and Entertainment		
Educational Expenses		
Child Care		
Other Expenses		
Total Expenses: $		
Summary:		
Total Income		
Minus Total Expenses	−	−
CASH FLOW (Is there a Surplus (+) or Deficit (-)?)	$	$

* Be sure the total payment includes the interest amount.

EXERCISE NO. 14b

Prepare Your Balance Sheet

ASSETS AS OF _____	$ Value (1)	$ Value (2)
Cash (Checking/Savings/Money Markets)		
Certificates of Deposit		
U.S. Savings Bonds		
Other Savings (T-Bills)		
Stocks & Bonds		
Mutual Fund Shares		
Market Value of Personal & Vacation Home		
Market Value of Investment Real Estate		
Surrender Value of Annuities		
Equity in Pension/Profit Sharing Plans		
Market Value of 401k/IRA/Keogh Plan		
Cash Value on Life Insurance		
Loans Receivable		
Personal Property:		
▪ Automobiles		
▪ Household Furnishings/Appliances		
▪ Collectibles & Antiques		
▪ Furs and Jewelry		
▪ Other Personal Property		
Other Assets		
Total Assets: $		
LIABILITIES		
Balance of Personal/Vacation Home Mortgage		
Balance due on Home Equity Loan		
Personal Loans		
Margin Loans		
Mortgage on Investment Properties		
Other Investment Loans		
Auto Loans		
Projected Tax Liability		
Other Liabilities		
Total Liabilities: $		
NET WORTH (Assets less Liabilities)		
NET WORTH (Assets less Personal and Vacation Home and Personal Property less Liabilities)		

www.wealthmentality.com

Ever hear the statement "Information is power"? That statement is simply not true. Information alone is not power. Getting information is only the first step toward having power. *Knowing what to do with the information* and then acting on the information is power.

Now that you have the information about the current status of your personal finances, what do you do with it? Below are the most important items to examine regularly to monitor progress and adjust your efforts as needed. Some of the items are ratios. Ratios are computations of relationships between various income statement and balance sheet items. Potential lenders use ratios when determining your credit worthiness. Some of the ratios discussed below are usually applied to business financial statements. I apply them personally because I think it is a good practice to view your personal wealth development as a business.

Income Statement

- **Cash Flow**

This figure represents how much money you have left after expenses to be used for improving your overall financial picture. You have two basic methods to improve your cash flow: increase your income or decrease your expenses. You can focus on doing both. Your goal here is to increase this figure.

- **Cash Flow to Income Ratio**

I've adopted the principles of this ratio from the business "Operating Income to Sales" ratio. The cash flow to income ratio is important because it measures how much of your income is exposed to expenses. Put another way, it measures how much of your cash flow is affected by decreases in income or increases in expenses. It is calculated by dividing cash flow by income. A ratio of less than 5% (.05) suggests that you have little or no room to react to a decrease in income or an increase in expenses. Your goal here is to increase this ratio.

- **Income to Interest Ratio**

This ratio measures how much of your income goes to pay interest expenses. It is calculated by dividing income by interest expense. A ratio of less than 1.0 indicates that you need more income just to cover interest payments. You want to have income that is several times your interest payments. Thus, your goal here is to increase this ratio.

Balance Sheet

- **Net Worth**

The figure for net worth in column (1) is what potential lenders will look at when determining your credit worthiness. However, for the purpose of developing a *Wealth Mentality* and achieving wealth, focus on the figure in column (2). Developing wealth requires that you turn your earned income into assets that produce passive income for you. If your personal residence and personal property does not produce income for you, then they do not increase your real wealth and you should not view them as a source of your wealth. Your goal here is to increase this figure.

- **Debt to Equity Ratio**

This ratio measures how much you have financed your lifestyle and/or investments with debt. It is calculated by dividing liabilities by the sum of liabilities and equity. This ratio is important to you and lenders because it gives an idea of your ability to cover your expenses if your income decreases. Your goal here is to decrease this ratio.

- **Assets to Liabilities Ratio**

This ratio measures your ability to pay your liabilities as they come due. It is calculated by dividing assets by liabilities. A ratio of less than 2.0 suggests that you are having difficulty meeting your liability expenses as they come due. Your goal here is to increase this ratio. However, a very high ratio may suggest that you are not making the best use of your cash by turning it into income producing assets. Thus, while your goal is to increase this ratio, just how high you increase it is a personal decision.

Why Spend Time Calculating Ratios?

I once was told by a seminar participant, "I can look at the statement and see that I have no money left after expenses." This may be true. However, I believe it is important to calculate ratios because they are specific and objective. Ratios provide a specific basis to measure and compare your progress. Ratios are objective in that they look at the whole picture and do not place a greater or lesser value on any one item on the income statement or balance sheet. It is possible for a person with a $25,000 yearly income to have the same or better ratios than a person with a $100,000 yearly income. It is possible to have a positive or even a very high net worth, but have negative cash flow. Conversely, it is possible to have positive or very high cash flow, but little or negative net worth.

You should learn about other ratios that are used to evaluate a business' financial standing. Experiment with other ratios by applying them to your personal finances. Doing this will allow you to measure your progress in a variety of ways and enable you to become more practiced and comfortable with using these tools for analyzing investment opportunities.

EXERCISE NO. 14c

Calculate Your Ratios

Using the information from your Income Statement and Balance Sheet, determine the following figures and ratios discussed above and measure your progress.

INCOME STATEMENT ITEMS*	As of ___	3 mos. Later	6 mos. Later	1 year later
Cash Flow				
Cash Flow to Income Ratio				
Income to Interest Ratio				

BALANCE SHEET ITEMS*	As of ___	3 mos. Later	6 mos. Later	1 year later
Net Worth				
Debt to Equity ratio				
Assets to Liabilities ratio				

* Use the extra rows to practice using other ratios for particular items that you want to focus on.

KEY POINTS

Part of having a *Wealth Mentality* includes knowing your current financial picture. A *Wealth Mentality* is able to prepare a personal income statement and balance sheet. A *Wealth Mentality* understands the importance of specifically and objectively measuring wealth development progress, and is able to identify and calculate the following:

- Cash Flow
- Cash Flow to Income Ratio
- Income to Interest Ratio
- Net Worth
- Debt to Equity Ratio
- Assets to Liabilities Ratio

STEP FIFTEEN

Bringing It All Together
Preparing to Seek Specific Wealth Building Information

Things may come to those who wait, but only those things left by those who hustle.
            Abraham Lincoln, 16th President of the USA

Now that you've determined your financial standing and how much wealth you want, it's time to start putting together your *Wealth Action Plan*. Putting together your *Wealth Action Plan* will require that you set goals, develop a financial education program, proactively seek "Gooses," get professional advice, increase the value you provide, choose role models, give to others, update, and revise.

Setting Your Goals

To set your goals, you need to ask: what is it that you really want to accomplish?

When doing this, separate the "need to's" from the "want to's" and the "nice to's." Set goals that are realistic and measurable. Make sure you have included time frames within which you want to achieve the goals. Your *Wealth Action Plan* should include goals in at least these six areas:

- Giving
- Educating yourself and your children
- Eliminating debt
- Beginning your own business (if you're so inclined) and/or investing in other businesses
- Attaining lifestyle desires; and
- Achieving financial independence.

Whatever it is you want to accomplish financially, you need to put these goals in a priority order. If you do not put your goals in priority order, you will be like the guy with the spinning plates who used to appear on the Ed Sullivan show. Everybody thought he was so terrific because he kept 10 plates and sticks spinning for quite a long time. That's what happens when you give equal priority to each goal, or each plate. Nothing ever gets finished and eventually, the plates come crashing to the ground.

If you're having trouble deciding what to work on first, I recommend the following order to start with:

1. Controlling your spending

2. Building your savings/emergency fund

3. Eliminating bad debt

4. Paying the minimum income tax required

5. Getting appropriate insurance coverage

6. Building your credit

7. Evaluating investment options

8. Developing a retirement plan; and

9. Developing an estate plan.

Controlling Your Spending

To control your spending, do the following:

- Stop the bleeding by eliminating impulse purchases and frivolous spending.

- Determine and remain focused on your priorities. Your money will always flow to your priorities, whatever they are.

Track your spending to be sure that you are directing your money toward achieving your goals. If you can't manage the money you have now, you won't be any better at managing more of it.

Here are two specific things you can do to take to control of your spending:

1. Categorize your activities as either income or expense activities. When you do this, the job of separating the important activities from the unimportant activities will become easier.

2. For your expense items, ask yourself how many hours of your life did you give up working for that expense. When you use a credit card, you are mortgaging your time. How much of your time have you mortgaged? Once you absorb this concept, you'll be serious about honoring your goals and spending your money wisely.

Savings/Emergency Fund

A *Wealth Mentality* knows that saving is not dependent upon income. Start by paying yourself first. Most people pay everyone else first and try to save what is left over. You must learn to save first and live off what is left over. I know that's hard to do at first. You may think that you can't possibly stretch your money any further. If that's your case, you're going to have to make sacrifices.

Start saving no less than 10% of your income now. Increase this number as you eliminate any bad debt and increase your income. Develop an emergency fund with enough to cover at least six months of living expenses. Make sure your emergency fund is kept in a place that keeps you on a pace with or ahead of the negative effects of taxes and inflation.

Once you have developed an emergency fund, change your focus from saving the 10% to investing the 10%. When you only save, your money is struggling to survive the negative effects of taxes and inflation. Therefore, becoming wealthy simply from saving is not a possibility because your money is never working for you. Investing gives your money the opportunity to work for you and brings the idea of becoming wealthy within the realm of possibility.

Eliminate Credit Card & Other Bad Debt

Make a budget to get out of all bad debt. Remember, bad debt is money borrowed for something that has no potential to pay for itself. From this point on, make sure that you pay off everything you charge when the bill arrives each month. If you can't afford to pay it off when the bill arrives each month, don't charge it. The *only* exception for having "bad debt" should be when you have investment income that can pay for it.

Minimize Income Taxes

Learn how to keep more of what you earn. Get a great tax advisor who can help you develop strategies to take advantage of all the tax rules and regulations. You must consider the tax consequences of purchases and investments before the money leaves your hands, and don't get excited about a large refund check. A *Wealth Mentality* knows that a large refund check is a sign of bad tax planning. You have better uses for your money than to give the government an interest-free loan.

Obtain Sufficient Insurance

Insurance protects your assets from tragic events. Get as much insurance as you need. Insure everything that you can't afford to replace.

Standard insurance lore says that the odds of being disabled at some point are one in eight. That's more likely than dying of cancer or of being in an auto accident. At a minimum, you want to have health, life and disability insurance in place. You should also check into the appropriateness of long-term care insurance for your situation.

Life insurance should be able to cover funeral expenses, pay off all debt (including mortgages and estate taxes), secure college education for your kids, and provide for no less than five years of your annual salary. If you're single or have no one you want to leave your money, donate the insurance benefits to a worthwhile cause.

Build Your Credit

Let's face it. Life is easier when you have good credit. Chances are that your pursuit of wealth may require that you take on "good debt." Having good credit will make it that much easier to attract the best terms possible for the debt.

Investments

Consider all types of investments ("Gooses"). You can start by investing in a mutual fund. No two funds operate the same way. A financial advisor can help you select a specific fund that is appropriate for your goals and situation. As you develop your *Wealth Mentality*, you will want to seek other types of investments.

Ideally, you want investments that produce enough income to pay off any debts, provide for your lifestyle, and appreciate in value. Don't dismiss any type of investment just because you don't understand how it works. Take the time to learn about it. Give the investment full consideration before deciding whether or not it is right for your plan. Review Step Eight for tips on evaluating investment information.

Retirement Planning

Those with a *Wealth Mentality* can't imagine "retiring" from something for which they have a passion and is part of their "life's purpose." As they mature, however, they can imagine acquiring a passion for other interests and wanting the opportunity to fully explore them without any limitations imposed by their finances. Learn about all types of retirement plans that are available to you, and take maximum advantage of all tax-deferred retirement plans for which you qualify. Combining pretax money with the miracle of compounding interest can give you quite a nest egg.

Estate Planning

It is crucial that you work with an estate planning professional to put a plan in place to prevent the bulk of your estate from going to the government when you die. Why allow the government to take what you've worked so hard to build? Many of us want our families to have our wealth when we die. Set it up so they can get what you have without losing the bulk of your estate's value. If you don't want your family to have your wealth, make plans to leave it to some worthwhile causes.

Develop a Financial Education Program

Don't wait for some miracle or personal tragedy to occur to enlighten you on managing your money. Begin your educational program now. Learning should be a lifelong process. Write up an actual calendar for yourself. You can start the process by deciding which:

- Financial periodicals you will read.

- Financial talk shows you will watch on television and listen to on the radio.

- Seminars and classes you will attend.

- Social activities you will attend that will increase your awareness on economic conditions and financial topics.

Proactively Look for "Gooses"

As I said before, seek the investments that provide the golden eggs — income that keeps coming as the years go by. Keep your eye out for the "Gooses" and grab them when they appear.

Get Professional Advice

The world is full of resources to help you determine how to achieve your specific goals. I recommend that you seek professional advice to help you consider your options for achieving your goals and to help you implement your plan. The work you've done up to now (determining your current financial picture and deciding and prioritizing your wealth goals) will help a professional give you specific and personalized advice.

Make a good, honest assessment of your own abilities. Your investments are far too important for you not to have the best advice. While the technology is available to allow you to purchase stocks on your own, invest money into various funds, and provide dollars to "worthwhile" projects, work with professionals who know more than you do about these areas. Their advice should be considered *along with* all the information you get on your own.

As one consultant advised me, "Concentrate on your strengths. Do what you do well. Find others who can do well what you don't do well and pay them to do it." Interpreting numbers and other information for investments is as much an art as it is a science. Assigning useful meaning to information is a distinguishing factor and a large part of the value that great financial advisors should bring you.

Be open to and seek out professional counseling resources in all forms. Implementing all the *Wealth Mentality Actions* will lead you to referrals for these resources.

Increase the Value You Provide

If someone else employs you, you should seek to truly excel at the job you were hired to do. Stop doing just the minimum to get by. Seek whatever training you need to be the best at what you do, even if it is at your own cost.

The skill and habit of doing excellent work will be an asset to you in your next job or if you start your own business. After you become excellent at what you were hired to do, find new ways to be of additional value to your employer.

As an employer, I regularly see employees trying to compensate for or excuse their performance by doing things that were not asked of them. While these "extras" are appreciated on some level, I can tell you that they are not as valued when the person is not excelling at what they were hired to do.

When you find new ways to be of value, excel at those things too. Believe me, an employer with a *Wealth Mentality* will recognize and compensate you for your real "added" value.

Choose Role Models

In developing and implementing your *Wealth Action Plan*, it is helpful to consider the experiences of others. Role models serve as a guide for the behaviors and actions that will help you get the things you want, and as encouragement when you become frustrated or have setbacks. You can build on their successes, learn from their mistakes, and take comfort from knowing that if they were able to rise above their circumstances, you can too.

Give, Give, Give

The great industrialist and philanthropist Andrew Carnegie gave away 350 million dollars. In his 1889 "Gospel of Wealth," he said "the man who dies … rich dies disgraced."

Whether you realize it or not at this point, the ultimate aim of all wealth is to share it with others. Share what you have earned, share what you have learned, and share yourself.

When you find yourself with the wealth you've always wanted, remember that you didn't do it alone. There were others who were there when your soul wasn't willing; others who gave you valuable experience, advice and knowledge and didn't accept a penny for it. The world provided an opportunity to be wealthy. When you become wealthy, you have an obligation to give back. And giving back pays dividends far beyond tangible measurement.

www.wealthmentality.com

Update, Revise, Update, Revise

Your *Wealth Action Plan*, like the world itself, is subject to the constant changes taking place. It is a living, breathing document. It will grow and evolve if carefully nurtured.

As you take action on your plan and maintain your educational program, you will constantly receive information that will influence your thoughts and change your goals. Children will be born, people will die, and friends and contacts will come and go. Therefore, you must periodically reexamine your *Wealth Action Plan* to test the validity of your vision, the value of your goals, and the effectiveness of your actions.

 EXERCISE NO. 15

What are Your Priorities?

In Exercise No. 14, you developed a vision of your future and made a list of the things you wanted to have, goals you wanted to accomplish, and situations you wanted to be in. Prioritize your list starting with what's most important to *you*.

KEY POINTS

To put together your *Wealth Action Plan*, you will need to:

• Set Goals – for all the important areas of your life. Prioritize them so that you accomplish the most important things first.
  - Control Your Spending
  - Save Your Money and Develop an "Emergency Fund"
  - Eliminate Bad Debt
  - Minimize Your Income Taxes
  - Obtain Sufficient Insurance
  - Build Your Credit
  - Invest Your Money
  - Plan For Your Retirement
  - Protect Your Estate

• Develop an Education Program
• Proactively Look for the "Gooses"
• Get Professional Advice
• Increase the Value You Provide
• Choose Role Models
• Give, Give, Give
• Update, Revise, Update, Revise

www.wealthmentality.com

STEP SIXTEEN

Setting Up a Wealth Mentality Club
Developing a Support System to Help You Along Your Journey

> *If you want to be successful and financially independent, practice the principle of 'O.Q.P.' (Only Quality People). Associate with people who have more than you and who know more than you because who you run with determines who you will become.*
>
> Les Brown, author of *Live Your Dreams*

Remaining on the path to wealth is not easy. Distractions, temptations and setbacks can make the journey at times seem lonely and very long. Having a support system is an essential tool for you helping you to maintain a *Wealth Mentality* and continue on your journey to wealth.

If you don't have an existing support system or if you would like to get to know other people who desire to develop and maintain a *Wealth Mentality*, then consider starting a *Wealth Mentality Club*. A *Wealth Mentality Club* works similarly to an investment club, but is broader in scope, as it deals with more than just stocks. It seeks to implement and build upon *Wealth Mentality* principles.

Here are some ideas for forming and maintaining a *Wealth Mentality Club*:

Who Should be Part of the Club?

The most important requirement for membership is that each of the members trust each other to be honest, helpful, and tight-lipped. Sensitive topics and information will be discussed during the club meetings. You will want to be sure that the discussions between club members are not repeated anywhere else.

Read Exercise No. 16 for initial steps in forming a *Wealth Mentality Club*. Additional resources are available on this book's web site. You may want to start by selecting two or three close friends and asking if they are interested in joining. Invite them to your home or another venue and develop some ground rules for the club.

One of the first orders of business should be for everyone to read and discuss this book in detail. All members should be ready to make periodic reports on their progress. They should also be willing to share information that has helped them develop and work on their *Wealth Action Plan*.

How Large Should the Club be?

The club should be as large as you feel it should be, but I recommend that you keep it at no more than 5-8 people.

What are the Aims of Such a Club?

The main aim of a *Wealth Mentality Club* is to provide support to those in the group. Following a *Wealth Action Plan* can at times be difficult to do on your own. It takes discipline and commitment. Having others "keeping you honest" often provides the reason to stay on your plan.

www.wealthmentality.com

Other aims are up to you. A *Wealth Mentality Club* can be an educational forum for exploring various wealth building vehicles and related topics. It can be used to investigate information members receive outside of club meetings. Members can help each other by setting goals each month or each quarter. You may find that individual members have their own weaknesses and strengths when it comes to staying with their individual plans. Another aim might be to have members use their strengths to help others with their weaknesses. It's up to you.

Should You Have a Regular Meeting Time?

Absolutely. Without a regular meeting time, the discipline of the group will fall apart. If any of you have ever encountered a Weight Watchers meeting, you'll know how important it is to have regular meetings and regular reporting.

An Investment Club Has Regular Speakers on Various Investment Topics. Should You do the Same?

Definitely. If you have the wherewithal to find speakers on wealth topics, feel free to have them come speak to the group. Otherwise, each member of the group can research topics and become the "expert" who speaks to the group.

What Should Happen at Your Meetings?

Again, this is up to you, but I recommend several regular items should be discussed. First, the members should report on how they are doing in keeping to their *Wealth Action Plan*. They should report on their successes and their setbacks.

Second, the members should report any other wealth building difficulties they have encountered since the last meeting. An open forum should be set up so that fellow members can advise the member on how to overcome the trouble or setback. Often, others have had the same experiences as the member.

Third, members should report on anything they've learned since they last met. This is the educational aspect of the group. It can be structured any way you like.

Should You Treat the Meetings as Social Gatherings, or Should You Maintain a Serious Tone?

By all means, have fun with your *Wealth Mentality Club*. If you have fun with it, you will be more apt to keep your interest in what you are doing. However, don't allow your fun to lessen the serious nature and importance of the meeting.

A *Wealth Mentality Club* is for the members to help each other grow their wealth. Always ask yourselves: Is this discussion or the action the club is taking good for the members? If it is not, don't do it.

EXERCISE NO. 16

Initial Steps in Forming a Wealth Mentality Club

a. Make a list of people who you think would be interested in developing and maintaining a *Wealth Mentality*.
b. Schedule dates when you can all meet and discuss, chapter by chapter, your individual interpretations and applications of the principles in this book.
c. From your meeting, you should be able to get a sense of who is willing to commit their time and energy to supporting one another in their achievement of wealth building goals.
d. Invite all such people to form a *Wealth Mentality Club*.
e. If you would like further guidance on how to set up and run a *Wealth Mentality Club*, obtain a copy of the "How to Start a *Wealth Mentality Club*" manual through this book's web site.

Epilogue

The only question with wealth is, what do you do with it?
John D. Rockefeller,
American industrialist and philanthropist

Since I began putting this book together, I have discussed the concepts in great detail with many people. I was amazed at how the idea of having a *Wealth Mentality* touched a chord in those I spoke to. I hope the idea of having a *Wealth Mentality* has touched a chord in you too.

By reading this book, I hope that you are now better equipped to develop and use a *Wealth Mentality* than you were before. I hope that the ideas in this book have inspired you to do some soul searching about the way you look at wealth. If I've accomplished anything, I hope I've encouraged you to think differently about the place of wealth in your life.

The accumulation of wealth, just for the sake of accumulation, is not the key to fulfillment. It is the way you use your wealth that can bring you fulfillment. As the great Spanish novelist and poet Miguel De Cervantes said, "The gratification of wealth is not found in mere possession or in lavish expenditure, but in its wise application." Applying the principles in this book to my life has brought me wealth and fulfillment beyond anything that I could have imagined. I hope the same happens for you.

Enjoy your wealth!

www.wealthmentality.com

ENDNOTES

Introduction

Statistic on lottery ticket sales: *Statistical Abstract of the United States, 2001.*

Who Wants to Be A Millionaire information: www.abc.go.com/primetime/millionaire/abouttheshow/facts.html

Author not available, *Singaporeans scramble for shot at "Millionaire" show*, Reuters 3-25-2001

Step One

Hammer story: Dr. Nancy Snyderman, *MC Hammer's Rise and Fall.*, ABC Good Morning America, 08-11-1999

Mandelbaum story: Jerry DeMarco, staff writer, *Retired Couple Suing Attorney in Ponzi Scheme.*, The Record (Bergen County, NJ), 8-21-1997.

Post story. Lois Gould, *Not a LOTTO luck. Pity the poor jackpot winners.*, Minneapolis Star Tribune, 05-01-1995.

Step Two

AARP Survey: Larry Lipman, Palm Beach Post Staff Writer, *POLL: ONE-THIRD OF AMERICANS FEAR WEALTH — AND DON'T WANT IT.*, The Palm Beach Post, 5-17-2000.

Step Eleven

Robert Allen quote in story on AT&T Global Information Systems/NCR: William J. Cook, Kevin Whitelaw, *Dialing for Dollars.*, U.S. News & World Report, 10-02-1995

Statistics in AT&T Global Information Systems/NCR: Author not available. *NCR gets name back as AT&T begins to spin off company it acquired in '91*. Minneapolis Star Tribune, 01-11-1996

Quaker Oats/Snapple story: Phyllis Berman, *Juicing it Up.*, Forbes Magazine, 05-18-1998.

Step Fifteen

Andrew Carnegie quote and story: Author Unknown, *Great Givers of Many Eras*, Time Magazine, 11-05-2001

ADDITIONAL RESOURCES

Want help putting the information in this book to use?

Visit this book's web site at
www.wealthmentality.com
What will you find?

Focus Topics

Objective and comprehensive information on different wealth building vehicles each month

Wealth Mentality Club

Resources, tools and tips for starting and building strong support systems

Wealth Mentality Book Club

Monthly recommendations of books and summaries that help you implement your Wealth Action Plan and maintain a Wealth Mentality

Wealth Mentality Newsletter

Monthly advice, tips and additional resources for developing and maintaining a Wealth Mentality

and much more wealth building information!

If you're looking for something that is not on the web site, please send me an email with your suggestion. I want wealthmentality.com to be your favorite wealth building resource!

NEED A HOBBY?

Do you enjoy cooking or gardening?

If so, visit with the author online at:

www.theparttimegourmet.com

and

www.theparttimegardener.com

Did you borrow this book? Want a copy of your own?
Need a great gift for a friend or loved one?

INVEST IN THIS BOOK

You can buy it from wherever books are sold,
copy and use the order form below, or call 800-962-6603.
- Please call for bulk orders -

ORDER FORM

YES, I want to invest in my future and buy a personal copy of this book.
I would like to order ____ copies of *Wealth Mentality*.

____ x $15.95 $_____
Plus $4.50 Shipping & Handling per book $_____
IL residents add 6.75% sales tax $_____
Total Amount Due with Order $_____

We accept checks, money orders, Visa or Mastercard.

Send my books to:

Name: _____ Ph: _____

Address: _____

City, State, Zip: _____

You can fax credit card orders to 800-962-0177

❏ Visa ❏ MC

Acct # _____ Exp. _____

Authorizing Signature _____

Mail order form to: **Jourdan & Brown Publishing**
104 W. Chestnut St. #101
Hinsdale, IL 60521

www.wealthmentality.com

INDEX

A
AARP (American Association of Retired Persons), 16 - 17, 35, 172
Allen, Robert, 120
AT&T, 120, 172

B
Balance Sheet, 141 - 142, 145 - 149
Barron's, 38, 80
Belief Barriers, 5, 55 - 63
Browne, Jackson, 32 - 33
BusinessWeek, 38, 80

C
Commitment, 99 - 100, 110

D
Debt, 73 - 74, 77, 141, 146, 148 - 149, 154, 161
Delehanty, Hugh, 17

E
Edison, Thomas, 107
Emergency Funds, 141, 153 - 154, 161
Estate Planning, 141, 153, 161

F
Far Eastern Economic Review, 80
Fear, 28, 30 - 32, 35, 42

Financial Plan, *See* Wealth Action Plan
Focusing, 99 - 110
Forbes, 9, 38, 80, 172
Fortune, 38, 80

G
Gates, Bill, 57
Giving (Chartitable), 17 - 18, 152, 160 - 161
"Gooses," 28, 33 - 35, 42, 68, 77, 83, 87, 90, 96, 98, 101, 151, 155, 157, 161

H
Habits, 113 - 118
Hammer, MC, 9, 10, 84, 172

I
Income Statement, 141 - 145, 148 - 149
Insight, 90, 95, 97 - 98
Insurance, 141, 143, 152, 155, 161
Investments, 141, 152, 155 - 156, 161
Investor's Business Daily, 37, 80

J
Jack and the Beanstalk, 33

K
Kipligenr's Personal Finance, 80

M

MADE Money, 68, 83, 129
Mandelbaum, Harry & Blanche, 10, 84, 171
Meditation, 99, 105, 110
Microsoft Corporation, 57
Mission Statement, 99, 101, 110
Modern Maturity, 17
Money (Magazine), 80
Murchison, Clint, 18

N

NCR, 120, 172
Net Worth, 144, 146, 148 - 149

P

Philosophy (Wealth Development), 99, 100 - 101, 110
Positive Affirmations, 99, 101 - 103, 110
Post, William "Bud", 10, 84, 171

Q

Quaker Oats, 121, 172

R

Rate of Return, 69 - 70, 76 - 77, 90, 96
Ratios, 93 - 94, 145 - 149
Redmoon, Ambrose, 58
Reminders, 99, 104, 110
Retirement, 141, 153, 156, 161

S

Savings, 141, 152 - 154
Setbacks, 5, 72, 119 - 124
Smithberg, William, 121
Social Security, 22, 38
Spending Habits, 141, 153, 161
Sullivan, Ed, 152
Survival Mentality, 37 - 38, 48

T

Taxes, 141, 152, 154 - 155, 161
The Economist, 80
The Financial Post, 80
The Financial Times, 80
The New York Times, 80
The Strategic Thinker, 82
Thought Barriers, 5, 43 - 53, 63, 102

V

Visualization, 99, 103 - 104, 110

W

Wall Street Journal, 37, 80
Wealth (definition), 15 - 16, 25, 128 - 129, 134 - 137
Wealth Action Plan, 5 - 6, 127 - 131, 151, 161, 164
Wealth Building Opportunities, 89
Wealth Development Philosophy, 99 - 101, 110
Wealth Mentality,
    Actions, 79 - 87, 99 - 100, 114, 117 - 118
    Book Club, 173
    Definition, 3, 11, 14, 41, 67
    Club, 163 - 167, 173
    Newsletter, 173
    Notebook, 6
    Thoughts, 67 -77, 79, 85, 87, 99 - 100, 114, 117 - 118, 120
Weight Watchers, 165
Wish, 28 - 30
Wish List, 34